The Easy, Easier, Easiest Cookbook

The
EASY
EASIER
EASIEST
COOKBOOK

Ruth Mellinkoff

Illustrated by Ray Skibinski

 WARNER BOOKS

A Warner Communications Company

Warner Books Edition
Copyright © 1980 by Ruth Mellinkoff
All rights reserved.
Warner Books, Inc., 75 Rockefeller Plaza, New York, N. Y. 10019

A Warner Communications Company

Distributed in the United States by Random House, Inc.,
and in Canada by Random House of Canada, Ltd.
First Printing: October 1980
10 9 8 7 6 5 4 3 2 1
Book design by Helen Roberts

Library of Congress Cataloging in Publication Data

Mellinkoff, Ruth.

The easy, easier, easiest cookbook.

Includes index
1. Cookery. I. Title
TX715.M513   641.5   80-15503
ISBN 0-446-51210-9

Contents

Introduction

The concept and contents of this cookbook are accurately reflected in its title. It is indeed a cookbook that provides recipes that are easy to do, demand no special skills, and can be speedily prepared. Should an unusually long time be needed for any recipe's preparation, it is a process that looks after itself—that is, only that kind of time that might be required for an unwatched pot. The recipes have then been structured according to a plan that further simplifies procedure, for each chapter has been arranged so that the reader-cook can quickly select what he or she prefers, according to a graduated scale of increasing ease of preparation.

This book is not for so-called purists. I do not believe that I have sacrificed taste; yet I have tried to keep an open mind and have experimented with all kinds of prepared commercial items. Some I have liked: dried and canned soups, bottled ketchups, mustards, tomato sauces and tomato paste, instant mashed potatoes. Some I found hopeless; for example, I inevitably could taste artificial and unpleasant flavorings in cake mixes. I have had no axes to grind; only palates to please. This is an iconoclastic cookbook that may not appeal to traditionalists but will, I believe, provide exquisite food for those who have neither the time and energy, nor the skills, nor the inclination for long and involved hours in the kitchen.

This cookbook is intended to be used as a primer or manual of convenient recipes. It is not a chatty cookbook. Instead, I have emphasized clarity of instruction and have added comments where appropriate about ahead-of-time preparation, along with occasional special tips. The recipes themselves are either innovations evolved from my experiments (planned and accidental) or they are variations of traditional dishes done "my way." What I would like to stress, however, is that I have cooked everything in this cookbook, including those recipes generously contributed by friends. And the specialties of my friends are among the best in the book; these are noted in each case by the name of the contributing friend in the title of the recipe.

To keep to the promise of simplicity, it has been necessary to eliminate certain kinds of preparations. There are no recipes for puff pastry or cream-puff pastry or in fact any kind of pastry. Nor are there any recipes for breads or coffee cakes made with yeast. Perhaps sometime in the future I will be able to provide new solutions to pastries and yeast breads too, but at present I do not think that any fall into the easy, easier, easiest categories I have bound myself to here.

Though this cookbook is planned for those with limited time and skills, it is focused on the universal desire to serve delicious and interesting food. It is in fact the result of my own changing needs. As my scholarly work has become more demanding and more time-consuming, I have determined to discover and uncover, to experiment and develop, new ways of producing superb cuisine that require limited time and effort. Imaginative cooks should use these recipes as an encouragement for inventions and variations of their own. Perhaps then all of us together can evolve a cuisine for our jet-age needs that is not only heavenly but divinely simple.

Important Preliminary Instructions Concerning the Use of This Book

1   Unless otherwise stated, oven temperatures are preheated temperatures.

2   Herbs listed in recipes are all intended to be read as *dried*, unless otherwise specified.

3   Parsley, green onions, and chives listed in recipes are all intended to be read as *fresh*, unless otherwise specified.

4   "Chicken breast" means one side of a chicken—that is, 8 chicken breasts would require a total of 4 chickens.

5   Canned soups listed in ingredients are intended to be used undiluted (even if condensed) unless otherwise indicated.

6   All measurements are level unless otherwise indicated.

The Easy, Easier, Easiest Cookbook

1/HANDY DANDIES

A pot-pourri of culinary advice, helpful hints, practical recipes, basic formulas, and a few magic tricks

HANDY DANDY No. 1

Garlic Oil

[the sine qua non *of easy cookery]*

1 whole head of garlic (at least 10 cloves), all cloves peeled
salad oil (any vegetable oil, *not* olive oil)

pint jar with a tight-fitting cover

Put garlic cloves through a garlic press or chop them finely. Put into the jar. Fill up the jar with oil, cover, and refrigerate. Use as needed: for recipes requiring a mere sniff of garlic, use oil only; use oil plus a little garlic for a bit stronger flavor; for recipes needing whole garlic, just dig down and spoon out some of the pressed garlic at the bottom of the jar.

Ahead of time: This keeps beautifully for several months if tightly covered and refrigerated, though it rarely lasts that long. Keep the jar on a double thickness of paper towels to catch any drippings.

Tip: Uses for garlic oil and the pressed garlic: salad dressings, sauces, seasoning poultry, beef, and lamb.

HANDY DANDY No. 2

Shallots Preserved

[for instant use]

1 cup finely chopped shallots
salad oil (any vegetable oil, *not* olive oil)

pint jar with tight-fitting cover

Peel shallots and chop finely. Place in the jar and cover with oil. Cover tightly and refrigerate. Whenever a recipe calls for chopped shallots, dig down with a spoon and take out the needed amount. The little oil that clings to the shallots will probably not need to be drained off; if they are to be sautéed, the oil will be useful.

Ahead of time: These keep a month or more if tightly covered and refrigerated.

Tip: Since shallots are sometimes difficult to find, this is a splendid way of preserving them when you do find them. Chopped shallots can also be frozen, but then they are not available for instant use.

HANDY DANDY No. 3

Teriyaki Basic Marinade
[makes about 1 quart]

1½ cups soy sauce
1½ cups dry white wine
¾ cup sugar
2 large cloves garlic, mashed, or use garlic from *Garlic Oil, Handy Dandy No. 1*, p. 3

one 3-inch piece fresh ginger, peeled, sliced, chopped, or mashed

Combine all ingredients and mix well. Store in a jar with a tight-fitting lid.

Ahead of time: Keeps a month or more if tightly covered and refrigerated.

HANDY DANDY No. 4

In the Manner of Hollandaise

1 cup sour cream
1 cup mayonnaise

2 to 4 tablespoons lemon
juice (to taste)

Blend carefully, then heat gently. (Be careful not to overheat—to just under a simmer is plenty, then remove from heat and serve.)

Ahead of time: Can be combined days to weeks ahead, and heated just before serving. If made ahead of time, keep refrigerated.

Tip: Delicious and easy for any fresh vegetable or broiled fish. Also excellent served cold.

HANDY DANDY No. 5

Versatile Sour-Cream and Dill Sauce

[makes about 1 quart]

3 cups sour cream
1½ teaspoons salt
½ teaspoon pepper
3 green onions, finely
   chopped

1 bunch fresh dill, finely
   chopped (about ½ to ¾
   cup)
¼ cup white wine vinegar

Combine ingredients and spoon into a jar with a tight-fitting cover. Store in the refrigerator. This is excellent for green salad, sliced tomatoes, sliced cucumbers, baking fish fillets, an appetizer dip, sauce for boiled potatoes, raw mushroom salad, or mashed with potatoes scooped out for restuffing baked potatoes.

Ahead of time: This will keep ten days or so in the refrigerator.

Tip: Dill is sometimes hard to find; when you locate some, chop and freeze it as directed in *"Frosted" Herbs, Handy Dandy No. 6,* p. 6. If desperate, substitute 1½ tablespoons dried dill weed in the recipe.

HANDY DANDY No. 6

"Frosted" Herbs

dill	rosemary
tarragon	chives
sweet basil	parsley
oregano	other herbs of your choice

Strip off heavy stems and wash herbs carefully; drain, then dry on paper towels at room temperature for 2 hours. Freeze either chopped or whole. Chopped herbs should be placed in containers with easily removable covers so you can readily spoon out what you need. Whole herbs can be divided and frozen in plastic bags.

Ahead of time: Since fresh herbs (especially some of the more exotic varieties) are seasonal and sometimes difficult to find, freezing is the ideal way of achieving an all-year-round herb garden. Freeze them when you can find them, or, if you have a garden, when they are at their fullest and best.

Tips—and Other Freezer Don't Forgets

1 Remember that hard cheeses freeze extremely well. I freeze some that are difficult to find or that I happen to get a good buy on, for example, imported parmesan. I buy it in 3- to 5-pound quantities and store some in chunks in the refrigerator (well wrapped, to be sure); some I grate and store in the freezer in plastic containers.

2 Buy shelled nuts when they first come in fresh (mostly in late autumn) and freeze them—always then available at their freshest for eating and baking (no rancid nuts) when you want them.

3 Buy candied fruit in autumn (around fruit-cake baking time when it is probably freshest) and store some in the freezer for all-year-round use.

4 Dried prunes, apricots, and other dried fruits will last beautifully fresh if kept in the freezer.

5 Foods in sauce keep better in the freezer than do those not so immersed; this also applies to sauces and soups.

HANDY DANDY No. 7

French Dressing (Vinaigrette)

3 teaspoons salt
½ teaspoon black pepper
1 teaspoon dry mustard
2 teaspoons sugar
   (irreverent, I know, but
   it improves the flavor)

1 or 2 garlic cloves,
   mashed, or use garlic
   from *Garlic Oil, Handy
   Dandy No. 1*, p. 3
1 cup vinegar (or part
   lemon juice)
2 cups salad oil

Combine all ingredients except the oil and beat them together thoroughly. Then whisk in the oil. Store in tightly sealed jars in the refrigerator.

Ahead of time: This keeps very well for several weeks or longer if tightly sealed and refrigerated. If you use olive oil, bring the dressing to room temperature before serving and all cloudiness will disappear.

Tip: Try adding 1 or 2 teaspoons of Worcestershire sauce—equally irreverent as adding sugar, and not very French—but good nevertheless.

HANDY DANDY No. 8

Russian Dressing

[multi-purpose]

1 cup mayonnaise
¼ cup ketchup (Heinz)
¼ cup chili sauce (Heinz)
2 teaspoons Dijon-type
   mustard
2 teaspoons grated
   horseradish (bottled)

1 teaspoon Worcestershire
   sauce (optional)
2 teaspoons red wine
   vinegar
dash of Tabasco sauce

optional additions:
2 hard-cooked eggs,
   mashed or chopped
3 green onions, finely
   chopped

¼ cup finely chopped green
   pepper
¼ cup finely chopped celery

Combine all ingredients (except optional additions); mix well, and store, covered, in the refrigerator. Use as needed.

Ahead of time: This will keep about a month in the refrigerator.

Tip: Add the optionals, if desired, a day or so before serving. The eggs are especially delicious, but any or all of the optionals are worth adding.

HANDY DANDY No. 9

Red Cocktail Sauce

[super-practical]

1 cup ketchup (Heinz)
1 cup chili sauce (Heinz)
½ cup grated horseradish
   (bottled)
   juice of ½ lemon (or
   more)

1 teaspoon Worcestershire
   sauce
a few drops Tabasco, or a
   pinch cayenne

Combine all and store in tightly covered glass or plastic containers in the refrigerator.

Ahead of time: Seems to keep almost forever in the refrigerator.

Tips: Lovely to have on hand for cold seafood such as oysters, cooked shrimp, cracked crab. Try it as a first course over cubed avocado. Also perfect with broiled hamburgers or to add to canned baked beans before heating.

HANDY DANDY No. 10

Remoulade Practicality

1½ cups mayonnaise (or part sour cream)

2 teaspoons mustard, Dijon-type

1 tablespoon chopped sweet pickles

1 tablespoon chopped capers

1 tablespoon chopped parsley

1 or 2 tablespoons chopped chives or green onions

¼ teaspoon basil

⅛ teaspoon tarragon

2 tablespoons lemon juice

Combine all ingredients and chill.

Ahead of time: Will keep in the refrigerator several weeks or longer.

Tip: This sauce goes equally well with cold or hot fish and shellfish.

HANDY DANDY No. 11

Tomato Sauce—Style A

[makes about 1 quart—
enough for about 1 pound pasta]

2 (28-ounce) cans tomatoes
1 teaspoon mashed garlic
   plus ¼ cup *Garlic Oil,*
   Handy Dandy No. 1, p.
   3

2 teaspoons basil
2 teaspoons sugar
   salt and pepper to taste

Combine and cook over moderate heat, uncovered, for about 1 hour or until somewhat thickened.

Ahead of time: This can be made several days ahead and stored in the refrigerator. It freezes well and is certainly "handy" to have just sitting waiting for you in the freezer.

Tip: If time allows, mash tomatoes either with your fingers or by putting them through a food mill.

HANDY DANDY No. 12

Tomato Sauce—Style B

[makes enough for about 1 pound pasta]

2 teaspoons mashed garlic
   and ¼ cup oil from
   Garlic Oil, Handy Dandy
   No. 1, p. 3
2 (6-ounce) cans tomato
   paste
2 cups water
2 beef bouillon cubes

½ cup dry red wine
½ teaspoon oregano
½ teaspoon thyme
½ teaspoon basil
2 tablespoons dehydrated
   minced onion
   salt and pepper to taste, if
   needed

Combine and place in saucepan. Cover and simmer for 30 minutes. Taste for seasoning.

Ahead of time: This can be made several days ahead and stored in the refrigerator; it also can be frozen.

HANDY DANDY No. 13

Self-Rising Flour

6 cups sifted flour (27 ounces)

3 tablespoons baking powder (combination type)

1 tablespoon salt

Sift or mix ingredients together. Store in a light room (not in a dark cupboard) in glass containers with tight-fitting covers (old mayonnaise jars are fine for this purpose).

Ahead of time: If stored as directed, this should keep well at room temperature for several months. And why buy a special self-rising flour for those special recipes calling for it when it is so easily and quickly made at home?

Tip: Flour, rice, beans, etc., keep best in glass containers where light can penetrate; this is the best insurance against weevils.

HANDY DANDY No. 14

Homemade Biscuit Mix

6 cups sifted flour (27 ounces)

3 tablespoons baking powder

1 tablespoon salt

1 cup vegetable shortening (8 ounces)

Sift together (or mix well) the flour, baking powder, and salt. Cut in shortening thoroughly. Store in a large glass container with a cover (or in several glass quart jars) at room temperature. Use as needed.

Ahead of time: This will keep at room temperature for several months. Really handy, and inexpensive too.

Tips: To make biscuits: For about 2½ cups biscuit mix, add ¾ cup milk. Knead lightly, then roll out to desired thickness, cut out biscuits and bake in a 450° oven for 12 to 15 minutes.

To make waffles: See recipe, p. 227

HANDY DANDY No. 15

Failsafe Rice

To cook: The real secret to perfect rice every time is to cook it like the Italians cook pasta: *al dente*—that is, barely tender; slightly resistant to the bite. It must never be overcooked. It matters not whether it is boiled, steamed, "risotto'd," or whatever; keep tasting and when it reaches the tender but still firm stage, stop the cooking.

To reheat: Nonsense it is that you cannot reheat rice! Witness the many variations on Chinese fried rice—made best, in fact, from cold cooked rice. But Chinese fried rice aside, I find that all types of cooked rice can be reheated perfectly easily. Place the rice (or risotto or whatever) in a heavy casserole (ceramic or Pyrex or enamel) and cover tightly (with a lid or with heavy foil or double foil). Preheat oven to 450°. Place rice in oven and immediately turn oven to 275°. Leave rice in oven only until piping hot. If it has been refrigerated, bring to room temperature several hours before time to reheat.

HANDY DANDY No. 16

Poaching Eggs Ahead of Time

very fresh eggs (the rule is: very fresh eggs for poaching, older eggs for hard-boiling!)

2 quarts of water
¼ cup vinegar
½ teaspoon salt
bowl of ice water

for later
salted water, just below
  simmering

The freshest of eggs should be used; the whites will adhere to the yolks only if the eggs are fresh. Combine the 2 quarts water, the vinegar, and the salt, and bring to a gentle simmer in a saucepan or skillet. Break eggs one at a time into a saucer and slide each into the water. Poach to desired state of doneness, then remove to the bowl of ice water (this stops the cooking and firms the egg). Trim the eggs and place them on a towel-lined tray. Cover and keep refrigerated. When ready to serve, place egg (or eggs) in water salted to taste and heated to just below the simmering point; heat but do not cook. Drain with a slotted spoon and use as wanted—as for example in Eggs Benedict.

Ahead of time: Any number of eggs can be poached in the early morning or even the day before. Just remember to keep them stored as directed in the recipe.

HANDY DANDY No. 17

The Magic Torch

Have you ever noticed that unlabeled bottle that the restaurant maitre d' (or waiter) has on his "cooking" cart as he is preparing flaming bananas or crêpes suzette? It's the *Magic Torch* that gives him his "magic touch." If you often agonize about whether to flame or not to flame because your attempts to flame cognac or other alcoholic liquids that were supposed to produce a beautiful burning have so often failed, even after you had tenderly and carefully warmed the liquor, relax, learn now; just buy the *Magic Torch:* 151 proof rum. It will even flame on ice.

No need to heat cognac or the Grand Marnier or whatever. No matter what dish you are preparing—main course or dessert—just place 1 or 2 ounces of this wonderful *Magic Torch* (rum) in a small glass, cover it tightly with plastic or foil, and put it in an inconspicuous place on your "flaming" tray along with the other liqueurs you plan to use. After you have added those—that is, at the very last—add this high-proof magic and flame away. (Don't overdo it, at least not until you become well acquainted with its burning qualities. Don't set yourself or your house on fire!)

Tip: And here is another lovely mini-handy-dandy for a flaming decoration—though not for eating: Should you want to present a "flaming" cake or dessert, such as Baked Alaska, surround (or top) it with sugar cubes that have been soaked in commercial lemon extract; light them and let them burn away. Very pretty and ever so easy and practical.

HANDY DANDY No. 18

Whipped Cream Immobilized

This is all about how to avoid the worry of whipped cream separating into a whipped lovely on top but a watery mess on the bottom! No need to face that unhappy prospect if you know the culinary simple secret—*stabilize it*. And stabilize it without anyone knowing what you have done; no taste change and no texture change. The miracle is achieved by using a small amount of unflavored powdered gelatin in the proportion of:

1 cup whipping cream: ½ teaspoon gelatin soaked in 1 tablespoon cold water

2 cups whipping cream: 1 teaspoon gelatin soaked in 2 tablespoons cold water

6 cups whipping cream: 1 tablespoon (1 package) gelatin soaked in ¼ cup plus 2 tablespoons cold water

These proportions are just right; do not alter them, and especially *do not use more gelatin*. The idea is to stabilize, not to jell. It is important to avoid even a hint of jelling of the cream.

And here is how to: Soak the gelatin in the cold water for about 5 minutes. Then dissolve (that is, melt) the soaked gelatin by placing it (in its container) over a small pot of simmering water. Whip the cream until barely stiff. Do not overwhip. Add the melted gelatin all at once to the whipped cream, beating simultaneously but only for a few seconds—just long enough to incorporate the gelatin. Then just go about your business—serve it in a bowl (with a dessert) or happily use it for decorating. Know that pleasant and comfortably secure feeling that all goes and will go well with your immobilized but perfect whipped cream.

HANDY DANDY No. 19

Nonesuch Cherries

[exotic emergency fare]

3 quarts fresh Bing cherries, pitted (12 cups)
3 to 4 cups sugar
1½ cups cognac or fine-quality California brandy

Combine all ingredients in one large bowl (or put combined ingredients into several smaller bowls). Place in refrigerator and stir occasionally (every other day or so) until the sugar has dissolved, then place in pint jars with tight-fitting covers and store in the refrigerator.

Ahead of time: The cherries will keep in the refrigerator a year or more.

Tip: These are well worth your time. Make the mixture at your leisure some evening when cherries are in season and you will be paid back a hundred times for the effort. Use in the winter to add to a dessert bowl of sliced oranges and bananas; or slightly thickened and heated as a sauce; as cherries for Cherries Jubilee; or as a warm sauce for baked ham or duckling; or for many other lovely dishes you will surely dream up.

HANDY DANDY No. 20

Brandied Bing Cherries

[more effortless elegance]

3 cups sugar
1 cup water
1 piece (1 inch) vanilla bean (optional)
good-quality California brandy (1½ cups to each cup syrup)
large perfect Bing cherries with stems (about 1 pound)

Make a sugar syrup by cooking the sugar with the water and vanilla (if used). Bring to a boil slowly, stirring constantly, until sugar dissolves, then cook without stirring until syrup is somewhat thickened. Cool slightly, then combine with the brandy at a ratio of 1 cup syrup to 1½ cups brandy.

Prick each cherry in several places with a fine skewer or a needle. Place the cherries, stem side up, in sterilized jars. Pour the brandy-syrup mixture over the cherries up to the top of each jar—the cherries must be covered. Seal and let jars stand for a minimum of 6 months before using; longer is better. Store on a shelf where there is not too much heat.

Ahead of time: They get better and better as the years go by.

Tip: Serve in small cups (or small glasses) with demitasse spoons as an elegant after-dinner surprise.

HANDY DANDY No. 21

Apricot Preserves

[makes about 4 cups]

1 pound dried apricots   ¾ cup sugar (or to taste)
2½ cups water

Simmer the apricots in the water in a covered saucepan for about ½ hour, or until quite soft. The water should be almost absorbed but the apricots still juicy. Mash the apricots, but do not purée unless you want to use all as a purée. Add ¾ cup sugar (or more if desired), heat again, and stir, but only long enough to dissolve the sugar completely. Spoon into sterilized jars (or other sterilized containers) and keep refrigerated.

Ahead of time: These will keep under refrigeration for a month or longer. They freeze wonderfully and will keep in the freezer for a year or longer.

Tips: Don't confuse these preserves with apricot jam, and especially not with commercial jam. They are not nearly as sweet and they have the real, intense taste of apricots. Use cold or hot over ice cream, with baked apples, and as a filling for cakes, tarts, and coffee cakes.

HANDY DANDY No. 22

Ported Prunes

large dried prunes
good-quality port wine
jars with tight-fitting covers

Cover prunes with boiling water and let them stand for one minute, then drain. Place prunes in jars and completely cover with port. Store on kitchen shelf at least one week before using.

These make marvelous accompaniment for chicken, squab, duck, or turkey. To transform them into a superb hot appetizer, pit them, fill with toasted almonds, wrap in bacon, and broil until bacon is crisp. For a wonderful emergency dessert, serve them with sweetened whipped cream and some grated dark sweet chocolate.

Ahead of time: Clearly these are an ahead-of-time preparation. They will keep for months on a kitchen shelf.

HANDY DANDY No. 23

THE "NEW" MEASUREMENTS

**Metric is on its way—so, just in case,
here are some equivalents:**

Volume:

1 teaspoon	5 milliliters
1 tablespoon	15 milliliters
1 cup	250 milliliters

Weight:

1 ounce	28 grams
1 pound	454 grams

Oven Temperatures:	Fahrenheit (F)	Celsius (C)
Very slow	250–275	120–135
Slow	300–325	150–165
Moderate	350–375	175–190
Hot	400–425	205–220
Very hot	450–475	230–245

Casserole Sizes:	Metric Approximate Equivalent:
1 quart	1 liter
1½ quart	1.5 liters
2 quart	2 liters

Baking Pan Sizes:	Metric Approximate Equivalent:
8-inch (round layer-cake pan)	20 centimeters
9-inch (round layer-cake pan)	23 centimeters
10-inch tube pan	25 centimeters
9 by 14 by 2 inch pan	23 by 33 by 5 centimeters
10½ by 15½ by 1 inch jelly roll pan	25 by 30 by 3 centimeters
9 by 5 by 3 inch loaf pan	23 by 13 by 8 centimeters

2/ APPETIZERS AND FIRST COURSES

Easy

Simplicity Crab-Stuffed Mushrooms

[makes enough filling for 12 very large mushrooms or 24 small ones]

12 extra-large fresh
    mushrooms
1 (7½-ounce) can crabmeat
    (1 cup fresh crabmeat is
    even better)
½ cup mayonnaise
½ teaspoon salt

¼ teaspoon pepper
½ teaspoon mustard
1 teaspoon dehydrated
    minced onion
⅛ teaspoon powdered
    ginger
grated parmesan cheese

Clean the mushrooms and remove stems. (Save stems for another use.) Place mushrooms in a greased baking pan. Combine all remaining ingredients except the cheese and fill the mushroom caps. Sprinkle with the grated cheese. Place in a 450° oven on the top shelf. Bake 15 to 20 minutes or until hot and browned. Serve on small plates with forks. If desired, small mushrooms can be used and served as finger food with paper napkins.

Ahead of time: These can be assembled the day before, covered, and refrigerated until about 2 hours before serving. Bring to room temperature and proceed with the cooking.

Tip: These are great as appetizers, but also consider them for a luncheon or light supper dish. They are very good cold the next day.

Artichoke Bottoms Filled with Tomatoes, Celery, Salami, and Cheese

cherry tomatoes, quartered, or regular tomatoes, coarsely chopped
celery, finely chopped
swiss cheese, cut in ¼-inch cubes
kosher-style salami, cut in ¼-inch cubes

finely chopped onions
French Dressing, Handy Dandy No. 7, p. 7
large artichoke bottoms (freshly cooked or canned)

Combine all ingredients except artichoke bottoms, place in a covered bowl, and refrigerate. (I use about equal amounts of the filling ingredients.) Fill artichoke bottoms shortly before serving.

Ahead of time: The vegetable-cheese-salami mixture can be prepared the day before.

Tip: This is also very good as a light luncheon dish. And the filling is excellent served on Boston lettuce (or any other lettuce) instead of in the artichoke bottoms.

Simplified but Glorious Pâté Pangloss

[makes 2 small loaves—enough to serve about 20]

1 clove garlic, mashed, or mashed garlic from *Garlic Oil, Handy Dandy No. 1, p. 3*
1 onion, sliced
¾ cup butter (6 ounces)
1 pound chicken livers
1¾ teaspoons salt
½ teaspoon pepper
scant ½ teaspoon, each, thyme, oregano, tarragon

5 slices firm white bread, crusts removed
1 cup cream (light or heavy)
4 extra-large eggs
1 teaspoon soy sauce
2 tablespoons cognac (or California brandy)

Sauté the garlic and onion in the butter over moderate heat for 5 minutes. Add the chicken livers and cook ½ minute, then remove from heat. Combine the remaining ingredients and add liver mixture. Whirl in a blender in about four batches (or in two batches in a food processor). Mix well, then spoon into two very heavily greased pans, 3¾ by 7½ by 2 inches in size. Cover tightly with foil and place in a baking pan. Pour boiling water into pan until it reaches almost halfway up the sides of the pans. Bake about 1½ to 2 hours in a 300° oven. Cool on racks without removing foil. Then unmold and wrap first in plastic, then in foil. Chill thoroughly.

Ahead of time: This can be prepared as long as 7 to 10 days ahead of time but must be kept very tightly wrapped and refrigerated; once unwrapped it should be eaten promptly. Keep unused portion wrapped and refrigerated. Since this pâté loses its lovely texture in the freezing process, freeze only to preserve leftovers for less festive occasions.

Tip: Garnish if desired with a generous topping of freshly chopped parsley. The pâté slices beautifully and makes a fine addition to a "French" lunch. Serve with chilled cornichons.

Lobster with Melon and Grapes

[serves about 4 as a first course;
2 or 3 as a main dish]

for the sauce:

¼ cup mayonnaise	1 tablespoon port wine
¼ cup ketchup	1 tablespoon Grand Marnier
¼ teaspoon salt	¼ teaspoon tarragon

2 cups diced cooked lobster	salt to taste
2 cups melon balls	juice of ½ lemon
1 cup seedless green grapes	

Combine sauce ingredients and chill. Combine the lobster, melon balls, and grapes with the salt and lemon juice. Cover and chill. Shortly before serving, pour the sauce over the lobster and fruit; mix gently. Serve on small plates.

Ahead of time: The sauce can be made several days ahead. The lobster and fruit can be combined the day before but must be kept covered and refrigerated.

Tip: This makes a delicious luncheon dish, but this amount would then serve only 2, or at most 3.

Brandied and Herbed Special Chicken Liver Pâté Nonpareil

[makes 4 or 5 small crocks]

2 medium-sized onions, sliced
1 clove garlic, mashed, or, better, garlic from *Garlic Oil, Handy Dandy No. 1,* p. 3
¾ cup butter (6 ounces)
1 pound chicken livers
1 tablespoon flour
1 teaspoon salt
½ teaspoon pepper
1 bay leaf
¼ teaspoon, each, thyme, oregano, and tarragon
3 tablespoons cognac or brandy

Sauté the onions and garlic in ½ cup of the butter until tender, then remove from skillet and reserve. Add the remaining ¼ cup butter to the skillet and sauté the livers until almost tender. Sprinkle with flour and add salt, pepper, bay leaf, thyme, oregano, and tarragon. Cover and simmer over lowest heat for about 1 or 2 minutes, or until livers are cooked. Discard bay leaf. Combine the liver and onion mixtures. Add cognac. Whirl in the blender (about one-fourth of the quantity at a time), then place in a bowl and stir well. Divide into crocks. Cover tightly and refrigerate.

Ahead of time: This can be made 2 to 3 days ahead. Cover each crock with plastic wrap, then with foil, and refrigerate. This pâté freezes beautifully.

Tip: It is difficult for me to choose between this pâté and *Glorious Pâté Pangloss* (p. 24). Each is excellent; this one has the advantage of freezing extremely well, while the other closely resembles a fine French foie gras.

Mushrooms Stuffed with Hamburger

[makes 24]

1½ pounds lean beef, ground twice
1½ teaspoons salt
¼ teaspoon garlic from *Garlic Oil, Handy Dandy No. 1*, p. 3
½ teaspoon pepper
¼ teaspoon thyme
¼ cup water
½ cup ketchup
24 fresh mushrooms (stems removed; save for another use)
melted butter

Combine the beef with the salt, garlic, pepper, thyme, water, and ketchup. Season the mushrooms by dipping them in melted butter and sprinkling lightly with salt and pepper. Place them open-side-up in a greased shallow pan. Stuff them generously with the ground-beef mixture. Broil for about 5 minutes (or to your taste). Serve hot. Nice to serve them topped with a dab of mustard or ketchup or sour cream.

Ahead of time: The mushrooms can be stuffed in the morning. Chill until 1 or 2 hours before broiling, then bring to room temperature.

Tip: These are also superb as a main course at lunch or supper (allow more per serving), and nice with something like creamed spinach and crisp toast or French bread.

Teriyaki Steak with Pâté

[makes 24 to 48 very small rolls]

*Teriyaki Basic Marinade, Handy
    Dandy No. 3, p. 4*
1½ to 2 pounds flank steak

4 ounces (about ½ cup)
    chicken liver pâté (see
    recipes, pp. 24 and 26
    chopped fresh parsley

Marinate the steak for several hours, or better, all day, then broil until rare or medium rare. Cool and chill. When cold, slice on a slant in very thin slices. Spread each slice thinly with pâté, then roll up slices and fasten with toothpicks. Dip in chopped parsley, then cover and refrigerate until near time to serve. Can be served icy cold or at room temperature.

Ahead of time: The steak can be marinated and broiled the day before. The rolls can be assembled in the morning and refrigerated, covered with plastic wrap, until serving time.

Tip: This works equally well with leftover rare roast beef, especially with a tender cut.

Bold, Rolled, Cold Omelets Filled with Pâté

[serves about 8]

6 eggs
4 teaspoons water
    salt and pepper
2 to 4 tablespoons butter
3 to 4 ounces (about ½ cup)
    chicken liver pâté (see
    recipes, p. 24 and p. 26
    or canned pâté de foie
    gras

½ cup mayonnaise
2 teaspoons Pick-a-Pecka or
    A-1 steak sauce
chopped parsley or
    chopped pistachios

Make two omelets, each with 3 eggs plus 2 teaspoons water and salt and pepper. Use about 1 or 2 tablespoons butter for each in a Teflon skillet with an 8-inch-diameter bottom. Cook omelets very slowly, but thoroughly, on one side only, then slide them onto plates to cool. Spread each generously with the pâté and roll up like jelly rolls. Combine the mayonnaise with either the Pick-a-Pecka or A-1 and cover the tops and sides of the omelets. Garnish with chopped parsley or chopped pistachios. Cover with plastic wrap and chill until time to serve. Slice and arrange on small plates and accompany with cherry tomatoes and cornichons.

Ahead of time: These can be made in the morning. Refrigerate until time to serve. Any leftovers are still delicious the next day.

Barbecued or Broiled Shrimp Ne Plus Ultra

[serves 4 to 6 as an appetizer]

1 pound extra-large raw shrimp in the shell	¼ cup soy sauce juice of 1 lemon
1 small onion, sliced	⅓ cup red wine vinegar
1 (2-inch) piece ginger, sliced	½ teaspoon salt
	¼ teaspoon pepper
1 clove garlic, mashed, or garlic from *Garlic Oil, Handy Dandy No. 1,* p 3	1 tablespoon sugar
	1½ cups salad oil

Shell and clean the shrimp (this is easily done with scissors). Leave shrimp raw. Combine remaining ingredients and place shrimp in this marinade for at least 2 to 3 hours. Drain shrimp and place on metal or Japanese bamboo skewers, 2 to 3 shrimp on each. Place on a barbecue grill or under the broiler for about 2 minutes on each side.

Ahead of time: The marinade can be combined 1 or 2 days ahead and kept covered—either in or out of refrigerator. The shrimp can be added to the marinade in the morning; after marinating they can be skewered several hours before cooking.

Tip: These make a superlative main course for lunch or dinner.

Easier

Humus Tahini

[makes about 4 cups—enough for a cocktail party of about 25 to 30 people]

3½ cups cooked garbanzo beans (same as chickpeas; canned ones are fine)

1½ cups tahini paste (found in Greek, Arab, Armenian, and Italian markets, or can be ordered from them)

2 garlic cloves, mashed, or, better, garlic from *Garlic Oil, Handy Dandy No. 1,* p. 3

juice of 3 to 4 lemons

1½ teaspoons salt (or to taste)

½ teaspoon pepper (or to taste)

2 or more tablespoons hot water

chopped parsley

Put the garbanzos through a food mill. Add the tahini, garlic, lemon juice, salt, and pepper and stir well. Gradually add a little hot water until mixture is of desired consistency—smooth and easy to spread but not too runny. Spread mixture on a plate (or plates) and sprinkle with chopped parsley. Serve at room temperature with sesame crackers or Armenian cracker bread or with pieces of pita bread (Middle Eastern pocket bread).

Ahead of time: This can be done several days or even a week ahead and kept covered and refrigerated. It freezes beautifully; defrost completely and stir well before serving.

Tip: Olive oil instead of water can be used to achieve a smooth consistency, but it is ever so fattening. Instead, try coating the top of the humus tahini, when ready to serve, with some good olive oil before adding the chopped parsley.

Elianne's Oeufs en Cocotte

eggs
softened butter
salt and pepper

heavy whipping cream (or better yet, *Crème Fraîche*, see following recipe)

Generously butter individual cocottes (tiny individual casseroles). Break an egg into each. Season with salt and pepper. Dot each with 1 or 2 teaspoons of butter, then spoon 2 tablespoons of cream over them. Place in a baking pan and bake 15 minutes (or longer—to taste) in a 350° oven.

CRÈME FRAÎCHE

Combine 1 cup sour cream with 1 cup heavy sweet cream and place in a bowl. Stir until blended, then cover and leave at room temperature about 10 hours. Stir, then store, covered, in the refrigerator for about 36 hours before using. Should·keep 1 to 2 weeks in the refrigerator.

Tiny Artichoke Bottoms Filled with Humus Tahini

tiny canned artichoke bottoms
*French Dressing, Handy Dandy
    No. 7*, p. 7

Humus Tahini, p. 30
chopped parsley

Marinate the artichoke bottoms in the dressing (unless you are using marinated ones). Drain, fill with *Humus Tahini*, sprinkle with chopped parsley, and chill briefly.

Ahead of time: *Humus Tahini* can be frozen easily and successfully (see recipe). If you have some on hand, defrost it and fill the artichoke bottoms.

Artichoke Bottoms with Shrimp

baby shrimp (Icelandic type),
    cooked (or substitute any
    small, cooked shrimp)
*French Dressing, Handy Dandy
    No. 7, p. 7*

small canned artichoke
    bottoms, drained and rinsed
    in cold water, then drained
    again
*Red Cocktail Sauce, Handy
    Dandy No. 9, p. 8*

Marinate the shrimp in the *French Dressing*. Drain and spoon shrimp into artichoke bottoms. Top each with a dab of *Red Cocktail Sauce*. Serve as appetizers either in the living room with cocktails, or at table as a first course.

Ahead of time: Both *French Dressing* and *Red Cocktail Sauce* can be made days ahead. The artichoke bottoms can be filled, covered, and refrigerated in the morning. Top with the sauce just before serving.

An Exotic But Very Easy First Course of Melon, Celery, and Coconut

[serves 8 as a first course]

2 cups finely chopped
    celery
2 or 3 tablespoons finely
    chopped fresh ginger
½ teaspoon salt
6 tablespoons tahini paste
    (if not available
    substitute creamy
    peanut butter)

½ teaspoon basil
4 teaspoons lemon juice
2 ripe cantaloupes,
    quartered
1 cup toasted shredded
    coconut (canned is fine)

Combine the celery, ginger, salt, tahini paste, basil, and lemon juice. Arrange on cantaloupe quarters. Top each with coconut.

Ahead of time: Celery mixture can be combined the day before. Cantaloupe can be filled in the morning, arranged on a platter, covered with plastic wrap, and chilled until time to serve.

Tip: Canned tahini paste is available in Italian, Greek, Arab, Armenian, or other special markets.

Smoked Whitefish Salad

[serves about 10]

2 to 2½ pounds smoked
  whitefish (very carefully
  skinned and boned), or
  any other kind of
  smoked fish you prefer
2 cups quartered cherry
  tomatoes
1 cup mayonnaise
1 heaping teaspoon Dijon-
  type mustard

juice of ½ lemon
freshly ground pepper
a whisper of salt (may
  need hardly any—
  depends on the fish)
2 green onions, finely
  chopped
chopped parsley (for
  garnishing)

Break or cut the boned fish into pieces and combine with the to-matoes. Mix together remaining ingredients (except parsley), then gently blend into fish and tomatoes. Divide into portions on shells or individual dishes. Sprinkle with chopped parsley. Cover tightly with plastic wrap and chill until time to serve.

Ahead of time: Fish can be boned the day before. All can be combined and chilled the morning before serving.

Tomato Halves with Smoked Salmon, Red Caviar, and Fresh Dill

[serves 12 to 24]

12 small tomatoes
12 ounces cream cheese (4
  small packages)
 1 cup sour cream
 9 ounces smoked salmon,
  diced

4 ounces red caviar
2 tablespoons chopped
  fresh dill (don't
  substitute dried; better
  to leave dill out)
chopped chives

Peel the tomatoes (easily done by dipping them in boiling wa-ter). Cut tomatoes in half, place on a serving dish, cover, and chill. Whip the cream cheese, then gradually beat in the sour cream. Stir in the remaining ingredients. Taste for salt—it prob-ably won't need any because of the salmon and caviar. Chill. Before serving place a generous spoonful of the cheese-caviar-salmon mixture on top of each tomato half (allow one or two per guest). Sprinkle with chopped chives and serve cold.

Ahead of time: The cheese mixture can be prepared the day before. Tomatoes can be peeled and chilled in the morning. Even simpler, skip peeling the tomatoes; just cut them in half and proceed with the recipe.

Golden Nuggets of Chicken

[makes 18 to 24]

2 boned and skinned chicken breasts	¾ teaspoon salt
⅓ cup dry bread crumbs (commercial are fine)	¼ teaspoon pepper
	½ teaspoon thyme
¼ cup grated parmesan cheese	1 teaspoon basil
	⅓ cup melted butter

Cut chicken breasts in 1-inch pieces. Combine the bread crumbs, grated parmesan, salt, pepper, thyme, and basil in a bowl. Dip the chicken pieces in the melted butter, then roll in the herbed crumbs. Place them in one layer on a foil-lined baking pan. Bake in a 425° oven for 10 to 12 minutes—no longer. Serve hot with toothpicks, or with small plates and forks.

Ahead of time: These can be assembled in the morning. Cover lightly and leave at room temperature. When ready to serve, bake as directed.

Tip: These also make an interesting luncheon or supper dish; this recipe would then serve two generously. Serve on a dinner plate accompanied with a green vegetable and perhaps buttered noodles or whipped potatoes.

Hot Canapé Sandwiches with Anchovy, Cream Cheese, and Butter

8 ounces cream cheese
(room temperature)
¼ pound butter (room
temperature)
1 ounce (about ½ tube)
anchovy paste

whole wheat bread, sliced
extra-thin, and crusts
removed

Mix cheese, butter, and anchovy paste together. Cut bread into rounds or squares or rectangles and sandwich two together with a generous portion of the mixture. Place on a baking pan and bake in a 400° oven until they are very hot and bread has toasted. (It is not necessary to turn them, just shift pan from lower part of oven to upper part and they will toast top and bottom.) This filling is also excellent cold with crisp crackers or hot toast, or used to stuff crisp celery.

Ahead of time: This filling can be prepared in advance (a week or more) and kept refrigerated until needed. To freeze, divide into small foil pans or individual crocks and wrap well.

A Somewhat Exotic Mixture of Cream Cheese, Pecans, Roquefort, Dates, and Chutney

8 ounces cream cheese
1½ ounces Roquefort cheese
(or good-quality blue
cheese)
½ cup finely chopped dates

1 tablespoon lemon juice
¼ cup chopped chutney
1¼ cups chopped pecans,
lightly toasted

Combine all and serve with crackers, or use to fill celery stalks or green pepper pieces.

Ahead of time: This is best made 24 hours ahead. It will keep in the refrigerator for at least 10 days, and it can be frozen.

My Version of Liptauer Cheese

[makes about 2½ cups]

9 ounces cream cheese (3
 small packages)
½ pound butter (2 sticks)
1 scant tablespoon anchovy
 paste
1½ tablespoons drained
 capers, chopped
2 tablespoons finely minced
 shallots (see *Shallots
 Preserved, Handy Dandy
 No. 2*, p. 3

3 teaspoons caraway seeds
 (plus more to decorate
 with)
1¾ to 2 teaspoons best-
 quality paprika
½ teaspoon salt (or to taste)

Cream the cheese and butter together (easier if at room temperature). Add remaining ingredients and beat until light and fluffy. Taste for salt. Spoon into crocks. Decorate tops with caraway seeds. Cover with plastic wrap and refrigerate at least 24 hours. Remove an hour or so before serving time.

Ahead of time: This can be made 7 to 10 days ahead of time and kept covered and refrigerated. Can be frozen; first chill overnight in the refrigerator, then wrap in plastic and in foil and freeze.

Tip: This is also good with the addition of about 1 tablespoon grated parmesan cheese and about 2 teaspoons Dijon-style mustard.

Curried Crabmeat Balls with Sesame Seed

[makes about 36]

1 (7-ounce) can crabmeat, well drained	1½ teaspoons curry powder
⅓ cup chopped chutney	2½ tablespoons mayonnaise
¼ teaspoon salt	toasted sesame seeds

Combine crabmeat, chutney, salt, curry powder, and mayonnaise and chill. Form mixture into bite-sized balls and roll in sesame seeds. Chill until time to serve.

Ahead of time: These can be prepared in the morning and kept chilled. They can also be made a day ahead; but don't roll them in sesame seeds until the day you plan to serve them.

Easiest

Lazybones Cocktail Pizzas

English muffins
Garlic Oil, Handy Dandy No. 1,
  p. 3
canned tomato paste
thinly sliced mozzarella or
  swiss cheese

anchovies
salt and pepper
oregano

Split the muffins and spread each with a coating of *Garlic Oil*. Coat with tomato paste and cover with a slice of cheese. Top each with an anchovy and sprinkle with just a tiny bit of salt, some pepper, and a pinch of oregano. Place on a shallow baking pan and bake at 400° for 15 to 20 minutes, or until cheese is bubbling and is beginning to brown. Cut into quarters and serve hot.

Ahead of time: These can be assembled the day before or in the morning. Cover and refrigerate until an hour or so before baking. They can also be frozen before baking. Defrost for about 30 minutes, then proceed with baking.

Pimentos with Anchovies

canned whole pimentos, seeds
  removed
anchovies

olive oil
vinegar

Cut pimentos in halves and place on a platter. Top each with an anchovy (or half an anchovy). Sprinkle generously with olive oil and lightly with vinegar. Cover with plastic wrap and leave at room temperature until time to serve.

Ahead of time: These can be assembled in the morning; just keep tightly covered until serving time. They can be done the day before but should then be refrigerated overnight. For best flavor bring to room temperature before serving.

Tip: This is a beautiful appetizer to serve in the living room; it is a splendid addition to a buffet.

38 /

Cheese and Red-Onion Mix

1 pound cheese (monterey
    jack or cheddar), grated
1 small red onion, finely
    chopped or grated

2 to 3 tablespoons
    mayonnaise
½ teaspoon black pepper

Combine and chill. Use cold as a spread for crackers or melba toast, or spread on toasted bread or crackers, broil for a few minutes, then serve hot.

Ahead of time: Can be made 1 or 2 weeks ahead of time. Keep well covered and refrigerated. It can also be frozen.

Tip: A food processor would make short work of this whole thing, so if you have one, don't hesitate to use it.

Appetizers, Skewered

favorite salami, cut in ½-inch
    cubes
favorite cheese, cut in ½-inch
    cubes

giant-sized pimento-stuffed
    olives

Put a cube of salami on a skewer, then a cube of cheese, then an olive. Serve either cold or at room temperature on an attractive serving dish. Have some good mustard nearby for dipping or for spooning on the skewered appetizers.

Ahead of time: These can be arranged on skewers in the morning. Cover well with plastic wrap and keep refrigerated.

Cream Cheese, Chutney, Almond Super Easy

[serves 8 to 12]

1 (8-ounce) block cream
   cheese
½ cup chopped chutney

½ cup toasted almonds,
   coarsely chopped

Place the cream cheese block on a decorative serving plate. Cover top completely with the chopped chutney, then top the chutney with the chopped almonds. Serve with water crackers.

Ahead of time: This can be assembled in the morning, covered with plastic wrap, and kept in the refrigerator. Be sure to remove it about 1 hour before serving, otherwise the cheese will be too hard and cold to use without its crumbling.

Cheddar-Cheese Spread with Pecans

[makes about 4 cups]

2 pounds well-aged cheddar
   cheese, grated
1 large clove garlic,
   mashed, or better,
   garlic from *Garlic Oil,*
   Handy Dandy No. 1, p
   3
2 teaspoons dry mustard

1 teaspoon salt
1 tablespoon Worcestershire
   sauce
few drops Tabasco sauce
12 ounces beer (1½ cups), at
   room temperature
chopped toasted pecans

Place the grated cheese in a mixing bowl and let it stand until it reaches room temperature, then beat with an electric beater until smooth. Add the seasonings, then gradually beat in the beer. Store in tightly covered containers in the refrigerator. Top with pecans before serving. Serve at room temperature.

Ahead of time: This will keep for several weeks in the refrigerator and for months in the freezer.

Tip: This can be heated gently, stirred, and served on toasted English muffins—a superb Welsh Rarebit to have always on hand either in refrigerator or freezer.

Curried Tuna-Egg Pâté with Chutney

[serves about 12]

1 (7-ounce) can tunafish in oil (do not drain)
3 hard-boiled eggs
½ cup mayonnaise
2 teaspoons curry powder
½ teaspoon salt (or to taste)
1 cup chopped chutney

Combine all ingredients except the chutney and whirl in a blender or a food processor. Place in a dish or bowl and frost the top with the chopped chutney. Chill. Serve with water crackers or any type of unsalted cracker or with toast.

Ahead of time: This can be prepared 1 or 2 days ahead and kept tightly covered and refrigerated. Freezing is not recommended.

Dilled Crabmeat Pâté

[serves 6 to 10]

3 ounces cream cheese
¾ cup mayonnaise
1 teaspoon soy sauce
1 clove garlic, mashed, or garlic from *Garlic Oil, Handy Dandy No. 1*, p 3
2 teaspoons Worcestershire sauce
few dashes Tabasco sauce
1 (7-ounce) can crabmeat
2 tablespoons chopped fresh dill
salt to taste

Beat the cream cheese with all ingredients except crabmeat and dill. When smooth, stir in the crabmeat and dill and season to taste. Chill at least several hours; better overnight. Serve with crackers or toast.

Ahead of time: This will keep several days in the refrigerator. I don't recommend freezing, though certainly leftovers for family use can be frozen.

Tip: This can be used very successfully as an elegant stuffing for hard-boiled eggs. Fill egg whites with the pâté, then devil the yolks and use to decorate around the edges of the eggs. If that is too complicated, top each stuffed egg with a scant teaspoon of the deviled egg yolk mixture.

Hard-Boiled Eggs Hurray: A Four-Way Easy Array

[each sauce will cover 12 eggs, cut in half; 12 or 24 servings]

I. WITH A SPECIAL SAUCE

1 cup sour cream
½ cup mayonnaise

¼ cup Durkee's Dressing
finely chopped parsley

Combine the sour cream, mayonnaise, and Durkee's. Place the eggs, cut sides down, on a platter or plates. Cover with sauce and garnish with chopped parsley.

II. WITH A MUSTARD SAUCE

2 cups mayonnaise
2 tablespoons light vinegar
   salt to taste
1 tablespoon (or more)
   Dijon-type mustard

cream to thin
chopped chives or green
   onions

Combine mayonnaise, vinegar, and salt. Add mustard and just enough cream to barely thin mixture. Place eggs, cut sides down, on a platter. Spoon sauce over eggs and garnish with chopped chives or green onions.

III. WITH A CURRY SAUCE

2 cups mayonnaise
2 teaspoons curry powder
   (or to taste)

cream to thin
paprika

Combine mayonnaise, curry powder, salt, and pepper, and just enough cream to thin slightly. Place eggs, cut sides down, on a platter. Cover with sauce. Garnish with a light sprinkling of paprika.

IV. WITH A WATERCRESS SAUCE

2 cups watercress (stems
removed)—about 1
large bunch
1 cup mayonnaise
⅓ cup cream

salt and pepper to taste
¼ teaspoon garlic salt
2 teaspoons lemon juice
tiny drop of green food
coloring (optional)

Whirl watercress with other ingredients in a blender. If using green food coloring, add it by dipping a toothpick into color, then into dressing—thus avoiding a too vivid and unpleasant effect. Place eggs, cut sides down, on a platter, then spoon sauce over eggs. Garnish with some additional watercress leaves.

Ahead of time: All the sauces can be made several days ahead and kept refrigerated. The eggs can be cooked the day before. The egg and sauce combinations can be completely arranged in the morning—that is, sauce can be spooned on, garnish added. Just cover well with plastic wrap and refrigerate until time to serve.

Tips: An easy-to-make and beautiful-to-look-at array for a buffet—especially if you do all four. And an interesting color effect too.

Two more ways: Use *Sour-Cream Dill Sauce* and *Russian Dressing, Handy Dandy Nos. 5* and *8,* pp. *5, 8.* Each covers 12 eggs.

Celery Stuffed with Roquefort Cheese Mix

crisp celery stalks, 24 to
48
¼ pound Roquefort cheese

¼ pound cream cheese
¼ pound butter
salt if needed

Cream the cheeses and butter together. Taste for seasoning and add salt only if necessary. Stuff celery stalks, cover, and chill until time to serve.

Ahead of time: The cheese mix can be made 7 to 10 days ahead and kept covered and refrigerated. It can be frozen for months. Fill the celery no longer than about 5 hours ahead or it will get limp.

Tip: This cheese mix served with pears and apples and toasted water crackers makes an excellent dessert.

Crabmeat-Cantaloupe Deluxe

[serves 6]

1 pound crabmeat, fresh or canned
1 lime
1 lemon
1 cup mayonnaise
2 teaspoons curry powder
¾ teaspoon ground cumin

3 cantaloupes, cut in halves (if you like, peel the halves and scallop the edges)
¼ cup toasted pine nuts, or toasted slivered almonds

Place the crabmeat in a bowl and cover with juice of half the lime and half the lemon. Combine the mayonnaise and the juice of the other halves of lime and lemon with curry powder and cumin. Keep mixtures separate, cover, and chill. Chill the cantaloupes. About an hour before serving fill cantaloupe halves with the crabmeat and top with the mayonnaise mixture. Sprinkle tops with the pine nuts. Chill again until time to serve. (Or fill just before serving.)

Ahead of time: Mixtures can be assembled in two bowls in the morning, covered, and chilled until time to serve.

Avocado, Sour-Cream, and Dill Dip

1 ripe avocado, mashed
   juice of 1 lemon
1 teaspoon garlic salt, or
   better, garlic from *Garlic*
   Oil, Handy Dandy No. 1,
   p. 3

1 cup sour cream
⅓ cup chopped fresh dill
salt and pepper to taste

Combine, cover, and chill. Use as desired.

Ahead of time: This can be prepared the day before and refrigerated; it can also be frozen.

Tip: Lovely as a dip for fresh raw vegetables, such as cucumber and celery sticks, cauliflower, Chinese peas, or any others that appeal.

Whirl Spread

[makes about 1½ cups]

8 ounces cream cheese
½ medium-sized green
   pepper, coarsely
   chopped

juice of ½ lemon
1 (3-ounce) can anchovy
   sprats, drained
chopped fresh dill

Place everything except the dill in a blender and blend until smooth. Serve chilled with chopped dill sprinkled on top. Good with water crackers.

Ahead of time: This can be prepared several days ahead; keep covered and refrigerated.

Tip: If fresh dill is not available, substitute any other fresh herb, or use chopped parsley or chopped chives.

Chessboard Canapés

[makes 72 to 96]

extra thinly sliced brown
  bread
extra thinly sliced white
  bread
soft butter

½ pound inexpensive black
  caviar (lumpfish is fine)
½ pound sliced smoked
  salmon

Remove crusts from bread. Butter slices generously. Cover white bread with caviar; cover brown bread with salmon. Cut slices in quarters and arrange on large plates or platters in a chessboard pattern. Cover tightly with plastic wrap and keep refrigerated until time to serve.

Ahead of time: These can be prepared in the morning and kept refrigerated until time to serve.

Tip: For easier storage when space is short, arrange chessboards on several pieces of foil or plastic wrap to fit platters, then stack them one on top of another. Cover well with foil and refrigerate. To serve, remove one chessboard on foil at a time.

Monterey Jack Cheese and Chile Easy Appetizers

bread slices (good-quality
  bread)
softened butter
canned green chiles (seeds
  removed)

monterey jack cheese, sliced
salt

Remove crusts from bread slices and butter *both sides*. Cover one slice with chiles and cheese slices and season with a little salt; top with a second slice. Place sandwiches on a baking pan and cut them in quarters. Set aside until ready to bake. When almost ready to serve, place the tiny sandwiches in the upper level of a 425° oven and bake about 10 minutes, or until well toasted. If some of the tops slide off during the baking, no need to worry; just replace them as you arrange them on your serving tray.

Ahead of time: The sandwiches can be assembled in the morning, covered with plastic and kept at room temperature. They can also be assembled the day before, covered with plastic and refrigerated, but bring to room temperature before baking.

A Marvelously Simple Hot Bean Dip

1 (1-pound, 14-ounce) can refried beans
1 (7-ounce) can green chile salsa
½ pound jack or cheddar cheese, grated

1 red onion, finely chopped
taco chips (homemade or bought)

Combine the refried beans, the chile salsa, and half the grated cheese and heat until very hot. Place in a chafing dish and surround with bowls of the chopped red onion, the remaining cheese, and taco chips. Each person helps himself by spooning bean dip on chips and topping them with chopped onion and grated cheese.

Ahead of time: This can be assembled 1 or 2 days ahead and refrigerated. Heat and stir over lowest heat, then place in chafing dish to serve.

Heavenly Tortilla and Cheese Wedges

large flour tortillas
grated cheese (jack or cheddar)

salad oil

Generously oil a shallow baking pan (pizza pan or other). Place one flour tortilla in the pan and cover with grated cheese. Cover with another tortilla and rub salad oil generously on top. Place in a preheated 400° oven on the bottom level and bake about 8 minutes. Then move pan to top level of oven and continue baking until brown and crisp. Cut in wedges and serve at once.

Ahead of time: Prepare the tortilla-cheese "sandwiches"—as many as you like—in the morning and keep covered until time to bake.

Nachos Simplified

[serves 8]

4 cups taco chips
½ pound grated cheddar
   cheese
1 (7-ounce) can green chile
   salsa

¾ to 1 cup guacamole
   (homemade or
   commercial frozen)

Arrange the taco chips in eight individual casseroles. Divide the grated cheddar over the chips, then spoon salsa on each. Broil about 3 to 4 minutes or until hot and lightly browned, then top each with a spoonful of guacamole and serve at once.

Tip: To make this even simpler, prepare it in one large casserole and serve it on small plates.

3/SOUPS

Easy

A Superior Onion Soup

[serves about 10]

10 large onions, sliced	3 teaspoons B.V. (or similar
1 cup butter	meat extract)
2 (10½-ounce) cans	1½ cups dry white wine
condensed beef bouillon	salt and pepper to taste
3 (10½-ounce) cans	¼ cup cognac (or good
consommé	California brandy)
2 cups water	grated parmesan cheese

Divide the sliced onions into two batches; sauté one batch at a time, each in ½ cup of the butter. Cook gently until onions are a golden brown (not dark and burned). Place them in a soup kettle and add bouillon, consommé, water, B.V. and wine. Bring soup to a boil, then simmer gently over low heat for about 30 minutes. Taste for seasoning and add salt and pepper to taste. Add cognac (or brandy) and heat again for a minute. Serve very hot with plenty of grated cheese.

Ahead of time: This can be cooked the day before (or in the morning) and it does freeze.

Tip: If possible, preheat soup bowls.

Garbure

[serves 6 to 10]

1 cup dried lima beans, soaked overnight in 3 cups water
3 pound piece of smoked ham
3 boiling potatoes, peeled and cubed
4 quarts water
1 garlic clove, mashed, or better, garlic from *Garlic Oil, Handy Dandy No. 1,* p. 3

2 onions, chopped
4 carrots, chopped
4 celery stalks, chopped
½ large cabbage, coarsely sliced or shredded
¼ teaspoon thyme
½ teaspoon basil
½ teaspoon oregano
salt and pepper to taste

Combine the soaked beans with the ham, potatoes, water, garlic, onions, carrots, and celery. Bring to a boil. Add remaining ingredients, cover, and simmer for 2 hours. Remove cover and simmer for another hour or so. Taste occasionally for seasoning. Remove ham, dice meat, then return to soup.

Ahead of time: This can be made a day ahead and refrigerated—it is even better the second and third day. It freezes well.

Soupe de Poissons, My Way

[serves about 6]

3 or 4 onions, coarsely chopped
3 teaspoons mashed garlic and 1 tablespoon garlic oil from *Garlic Oil, Handy Dandy No. 1,* p. 3
½ cup olive oil
3 cups canned tomatoes
1 (8-ounce) can tomato sauce

2 quarts water
1 tablespoon salt (or more)
½ teaspoon pepper
½ teaspoon thyme
2 bay leaves
½ teaspoon fennel seeds
3 pounds fish trimmings from any variety of white fishes

Sauté the onions and garlic in the *Garlic Oil* and olive oil over moderate heat for several minutes—until lightly browned. Add remaining ingredients and simmer gently, uncovered, for 1 to 1½ hours. Strain through a sieve. Reheat, taste for seasoning, and serve very hot.

Ahead of time: This can be prepared the day before; it freezes well too.

Tip: This makes a fabulous base for bouillabaise.

March-Far-and-Long Borscht

[serves 6 to 10]

4 pounds beef pot roast (chuck, brisket or lean short ribs)
2½ quarts water
3 onions, coarsely chopped
salt and pepper to taste
3 cups canned tomatoes

1 (8-ounce) can tomato sauce
½ cup lemon juice
½ cup brown sugar
1 large firm cabbage, coarsely cut or shredded

Remove excess fat from the meat. Place meat in a large pot and cover with the water. Bring to a boil, add the onions, some salt and pepper, and the tomatoes and tomato sauce. Cover and cook very slowly until beef begins to get tender (about 1½ hours) but is not completely cooked. Add remaining ingredients and simmer uncovered for about another hour or longer—until meat is tender. Taste for seasoning occasionally, then adjust salt, pepper, lemon juice, and sugar. Remove the meat, trim it, dice it, then return diced meat to the soup. Serve in large warmed bowls, accompanied by quantities of rye bread and sweet butter.

Ahead of time: This is even better made 1 or 2 days ahead. Refrigerate, then reheat before serving. (It is much easier to trim and dice the beef after it has been chilled overnight.) This freezes well too.

Split-Pea or Lentil Soup

[makes 6 or more quarts]

4 cups (2 pounds) split peas or lentils, or half and half
4 quarts of water
2 teaspoons mashed garlic from *Garlic Oil, Handy Dandy No. 1,* p. 3
2 onions, chopped
4 carrots, chopped
4 celery stalks, chopped
2 tablespoons salt (or less if ham is salty)
1 teaspoon black pepper
ham bone (optional)
1 quart diced ham

Combine all ingredients *except* the diced ham. Bring to a boil, then lower heat and simmer until peas or lentils are very tender (several hours). Simmer most of the time with the pot covered. Uncover and simmer for ½ to 1 hour. Add diced ham and simmer another half hour. Taste for seasoning.

Ahead of time: This, like many soups, can be made ahead and in fact improves in flavor in the reheating. And it does freeze well.

Tip: For an elegant and unusual dinner, serve this as your main course along with a large bowl of hot, peeled, boiled shrimp. The guests themselves add the shrimp to the very hot soup. Nothing else is needed except French bread and a salad.

Easygoing Minestrone

[serves about 8]

4 (10½-ounce) cans
  condensed beef bouillon
5 cups water
1 cup macaroni
1 (10-ounce) package frozen
  peas and carrots
1 (10-ounce) package frozen
  spinach

1 (10-ounce) package frozen
  lima beans
salt and pepper (to taste)
½ small cabbage, coarsely
  chopped
grated parmesan cheese

Bring the bouillon and water to a boil, then add the macaroni and cook about 5 minutes. Add the vegetables and salt and pepper, then cook gently until macaroni is tender and vegetables cooked. Taste for seasoning. Serve very hot with a generous topping of grated parmesan cheese.

Ahead of time: This can be prepared the day before.

Tip: Don't hesitate to substitute your own vegetable preferences; you might like to add some onion and tomato too.

Mushroom Soup

[serves about 8]

1½ pounds fresh mushrooms,
  sliced
3 tablespoons butter
3 tablespoons flour
8 cups chicken stock (I use
  Spice Islands chicken
  concentrate combined
  with boiling water)

¾ cup heavy cream
salt and pepper to taste
chopped parsley

Sauté the mushrooms in the butter for about 3 to 5 minutes. Sprinkle with flour, stir, and cook 1 minute. Remove from heat and add 1 cup of the stock. Stir, then add the remaining stock and seasoning, then return to heat. Simmer gently for 10 minutes. Add cream, then heat but do not boil. Serve in warmed soup bowls and garnish with chopped parsley.

Ahead of time: This can be prepared in the morning or the day before, and it can be frozen.

Albóndigas Soup

[serves about 8]

1 onion, chopped
2 large carrots, chopped
¼ cup olive oil
3 (10½-ounce) cans consommé
3 cups chicken stock
3 cups water
¼ cup tomato sauce
1 pound lean ground beef
3 tablespoons raw rice

1 tablespoon chopped parsley
1½ teaspoons salt
¼ teaspoon pepper
1 egg
1 (10-ounce) package frozen peas
1 tablespoon freshly chopped mint (optional)

Sauté the onion and carrots in the olive oil. Add the consommé, chicken stock, water, and tomato sauce. Simmer for 15 minutes. Mix together the ground beef, rice, parsley, salt, pepper, and egg. Form into tiny meat balls. Bring soup to a boil, add meat balls, and simmer gently for 20 minutes. Add the peas and chopped mint (if used) and cook 5 minutes more.

Ahead of time: This can be prepared the day before and reheated before serving. It can be frozen; if so, freeze before adding peas and mint; defrost, add these, and reheat.

Clam and Celery Soup

[serves 8]

2 cups finely chopped
  celery
¼ cup butter
4 cups rich chicken stock

2 (6-ounce) cans minced
  clams
salt and pepper to taste
½ cup cream

Sauté the celery in the butter for a few minutes. Add the chicken stock. Drain the clams and reserve; add only the clam juice. Simmer for 15 minutes. Taste for seasoning. Add reserved clams and the cream and heat slowly. (Do not overcook or clams will toughen.)

Ahead of time: This can be prepared the day before and it can be frozen. Take care to reheat gently.

═══*Easiest*

Quick Lobster Bisque

[enough for 4 medium-sized servings]

1 (11¼-ounce) can
   condensed green pea
   soup
1 (10¾-ounce) can
   condensed tomato soup
1 (10½-ounce) can
   condensed beef bouillon

3 tablespoons butter
1 cup water or milk
   lobster shells (if you have
   any)
2 tablespoons madeira (or
   sherry)
1½ cups diced cooked lobster

Combine the soups, butter, water or milk, and lobster shells (if available). Simmer, stirring occasionally, for about 10 minutes. If shells are used, strain to remove them. Add the madeira and diced lobster. Heat gently; do not boil or the lobster will toughen.

Tip: This can also be made with shrimp. If you have shrimp shells use those instead of the lobster shells, and if the shrimp are tiny just use them whole.

Peggy Leavitt's Cold Clam and Cucumber Soup

[serves 4 generously]

1 cucumber, peeled and
   thinly sliced
1 (1-pound) can stewed
   tomatoes
1 (6-ounce) can minced
   clams with their liquid
1 (7-ounce) can chopped
   clams with their liquid

1 bunch green onions,
   chopped, not all of the
   green
½ teaspoon pepper
½ teaspoon salt
½ teaspoon dill weed
½ cup sour cream

Combine everything in a large bowl. Cover and chill for several hours.

Ahead of time: Clearly this is best made in the early morning or the day before.

Tip: This can be served as a first course, or in larger portions it might be nice as a main luncheon course on a very hot summer day.

Susan Grotstein's Copper-Kettle Consommé

[serves 6]

6 cups (uncondensed) chicken consommé
1 cup clam juice
2 bay leaves
¼ cup dry white wine
1 carrot, peeled and shredded

1 celery stalk (with leaves), thinly sliced
1 red or green sweet pepper, seeded and slivered
2 green onions (tops too), thinly sliced

Bring the consommé, clam juice, and bay leaves to a boil in a covered saucepan. Simmer 15 minutes, then remove bay leaves. Add the wine and heat gently. Divide the vegetables among six soup bowls and pour broth over them; serve at once.

Ahead of time: The vegetables can be readied in the morning; keep covered and refrigerated until 1 or 2 hours before serving (they should be at room temperature or they will cool the broth too much).

Tip: If you have the space, heat the soup bowls in a low oven or on a heating tray.

Marianne Birnbaum's Dill Pickle Soup

[serves 6 to 8]

1 (22–24 ounce) jar dill pickles (halved or quartered in the jar)
4 cups water
3 tablespoons dill weed
1 (10½-ounce) can condensed chicken broth

juice of 1 lemon
1½ cups mayonnaise
salt and pepper to taste (about ¼ teaspoon pepper and ½ teaspoon salt, but taste, because pickles are salty)
2 hard-boiled eggs, sliced

Remove the pickles from jar and rinse them once lightly with water. Drain. Separate them into two stacks. Place one stack in a blender and add 2 cups water. Whirl to blend and chop. Repeat with remaining pickles and 2 cups water. Place in a large bowl and add the dill weed, chicken broth, lemon juice, mayonnaise, salt, and pepper. Now whirl this mixture in two or three batches in the blender. Pour into a serving dish and chill—overnight if possible. Serve with sliced hard-boiled eggs (about 2 slices in each bowl).

Ahead of time: This not only can be done the day before, it should be done the day before.

Tip: Let your guests try to guess the ingredients; they will never succeed but they will enjoy this mysteriously delicious soup.

4/FISH AND SHELLFISH

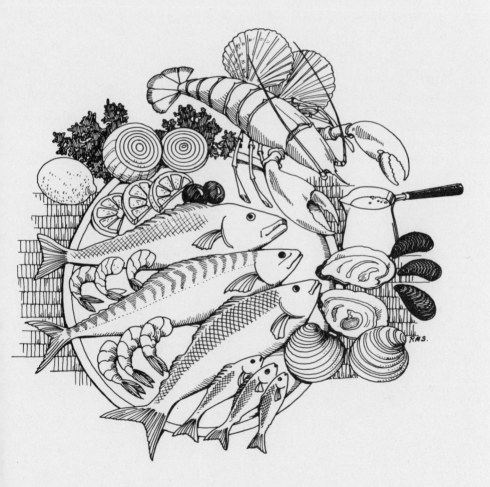

Salmon Steaks Sensational

[serves 10]

10 fresh salmon steaks (½ inch thick)
salt and pepper
juice of 1 lemon
2 tablespoons butter
2 tablespoons flour

1 teaspoon salt
½ teaspoon pepper
2 cups sour cream
2 onions, sliced wafer thin
3 green peppers, sliced in rings

Season salmon steaks with salt, pepper, and lemon juice. Place them in two large buttered casseroles (Pyrex, enamel, or stainless steel). Melt the 2 tablespoons butter, stir in the flour, and add the 1 teaspoon salt and the ½ teaspoon pepper. Add the sour cream and stir until it boils, then remove from heat. Arrange about a fourth of the onion slices and a fourth of the green pepper rings on the fish in each casserole; then spoon half the sauce on each. Top with the rest of the onion and green pepper. Cover with foil and bake in a 425° oven for 10 minutes. Remove foil and bake for about another 15 to 20 minutes.

Ahead of time: This can be assembled in the morning, then refrigerated. Bring to room temperature first, or allow more time for baking.

Joyfully Easy Salmon or Crabmeat Cakes

[serves 4 to 6]

1 small onion, chopped
1 green pepper, chopped
3 tablespoons butter
1 pound canned salmon or crabmeat
salt and pepper to taste
¼ teaspoon thyme

1 egg, beaten
1½ cups soft bread crumbs
3 tablespoons mayonnaise
dash of Tabasco
dry bread crumbs
oil or butter

Sauté the onion and green pepper in the butter until tender. Add the fish and stir over heat for about 1 minute. Remove from heat, add the salt and pepper, thyme, beaten egg, soft bread crumbs, mayonnaise, and Tabasco and mix thoroughly. Chill at least 1 hour. Form into 8 cakes and roll them in the dry bread crumbs. (If time permits, chill cakes again.) Sauté in oil or butter until nicely browned. Serve with *Remoulade Practicality, Handy Dandy No. 10*, p. 9.

Ahead of time: The salmon or crabmeat cakes can be made the day before, or in the morning, up to the point of sautéing. Keep refrigerated until ready to cook. They can also be frozen; defrost for about an hour or so, roll in more dry bread crumbs, then proceed with sautéing.

Mary Cullins' Oyster Loaves

[serves 6]

6 large French rolls (sour dough or any other kind)
1 pint fresh oysters

salt and pepper
flour
cornmeal
oil for frying

for the sauce

1 onion, chopped
1 green pepper, chopped
1 cup ketchup (Heinz)
1 teaspoon Worcestershire sauce

juice of ½ lemon
dash Tabasco

Cut a top off each roll and scoop out some of the soft part. Reserve the tops. Make the sauce: Combine onion, green pepper, ketchup, Tabasco, Worcestershire, and lemon juice. Bring to a boil and simmer for 2 minutes, then set aside. Season oysters with salt and pepper. Roll them in a mixture of half flour and half cornmeal and fry them in oil until brown and crisp. Drain on paper towels. Fill each roll with oysters. Spoon sauce over them very generously. Replace the tops, then wrap rolls in foil. Place in a 450° oven for 5 minutes, then take out and remove the foil. Heat another 5 minutes or so or until hot.

Ahead of time: These can be done either the day before or in the morning. Wrap in foil and refrigerate. Before serving first heat in the foil for 10 minutes at 450°, then remove foil, reduce heat to about 400° and heat another 10 to 15 minutes or until hot. They can also be frozen; heat without defrosting in the foil wrappers at 450° for about 20 to 30 minutes, then unwrap, reduce oven to about 400° and heat another 10 minutes or so.

Scallops Divine

[serves 6 to 8 as a light lunch or first course]

2 pounds scallops (if large, cut into smaller pieces)
2 egg yolks
2 teaspoons lemon juice
¼ cup dry white wine

4 teaspoons dehydrated minced onion
1¼ teaspoons salt
½ teaspoon pepper
½ teaspoon oregano

for the topping

1 cup soft white bread crumbs
2 tablespoons melted butter

2 tablespoons grated parmesan cheese

Combine the ingredients for the topping and set aside. Combine the egg yolks, lemon juice, wine, onion, salt, pepper, and oregano and mix well. Arrange the scallops in individual casseroles or on shells. Shortly before serving, spoon the egg sauce over the scallops and sprinkle with the topping. Bake about 12 to 15 minutes in a 450° oven (don't overcook).

Ahead of time: The sauce ingredients can be combined in the morning and refrigerated; refrigerate the scallops too, separate from the sauce. Bring to room temperature shortly before time to bake, then spoon the sauce over the scallops and proceed as directed in the recipe.

Tip: This can be successfully done in one large casserole—the ovenproof shallow kind (Pyrex, enamel, ceramic). I like these cold the next day, when I'm fortunate enough to have any left.

Streamlined Scampi

[serves 4 to 6 as a main course;
8 to 12 as a first course]

24 to 30 large or jumbo raw
    shrimp
salt and pepper
2 cloves garlic, mashed, and
    4 tablespoons oil, or
    better, 2 teaspoons
    garlic and 4 tablespoons
    oil from *Garlic Oil,*
    Handy Dandy, No. 1, p.
    3

½ cup butter, melted
4 tablespoons lemon juice
⅓ cup madeira (or sherry)
    chopped parsley

Pull the feet off the shrimp, then cut in half lengthwise, but do not cut through the tails. Place shrimp in one layer (they can overlap) in either a large shallow baking pan or individual casseroles. Season lightly with salt and pepper. Combine the remaining ingredients, except the parsley, and spoon over the shrimp. Bake in a 500° oven for 5 to 10 minutes—depending on the temperature and size of the shrimp. Do not overcook. Sprinkle with chopped parsley. If they are served from one large dish, be sure to spoon some of the sauce over each portion.

Ahead of time: Both sauce and shrimp can be prepared in the morning but do not combine them. Refrigerate separately until about 2 hours before time to cook, then bring to room temperature and proceed with recipe.

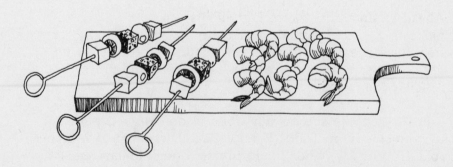

Seafood Salad Baked

[serves 8]

7 slices Canadian bacon,
  diced (optional; or use
  regular bacon)
2 tablespoons butter
¾ pound fresh mushrooms,
  sliced (optional)
1 pound cooked shrimp
¾ pound crabmeat
9 green onions, chopped
1¼ cups celery, chopped
1 green pepper, chopped

1 cup mayonnaise
3 tablespoons lemon juice
1 teaspoon Worcestershire
  sauce
dash of Tabasco
salt and pepper to taste
½ clove garlic, mashed, or
  garlic from *Garlic Oil,
  Handy Dandy, No. 1*, p.
  3

for the topping
½ cup dry bread crumbs
2 tablespoons grated
  parmesan cheese

2 tablespoons butter

Cook the bacon in 2 tablespoons butter for 1 minute. Add mushrooms (if used) and cook another 5 minutes. Remove from heat and mix with all other ingredients except those for the topping. Prepare topping by combining the crumbs, parmesan and 2 tablespoons butter in a skillet and heating slowly, stirring until crumbs are lightly browned—about 2 or 3 minutes. Place seafood mixture in a large casserole and cover with buttered crumbs. Heat thoroughly in a 350° oven—about 20 minutes or so if seafood was at room temperature.

Ahead of time: This can be prepared up to the point of baking the day before or in the morning. Refrigerate until about 2 hours before time to bake, then proceed as directed in the recipe.

Tip: Keep in mind that this can be doubled or tripled for something like a holiday buffet; and if you omit the bacon and the mushrooms it is mostly just an assembly job.

Easier

Ruth Benson's Delectable Baked Salmon with Chiles and Cheddar

[serves 4 to 6]

1 (1-pound) can salmon
1 (4-ounce) can green chiles (or more), seeded, then chopped
1 (10½-ounce) can condensed cream of onion soup (or chicken broth)
1 (6-ounce) can tomato paste (or about ½ cup tangy tomato sauce)
¼ pound cheddar cheese, grated
1 tablespoon onion powder
1 tablespoon garlic salt or garlic powder, or garlic from *Garlic Oil, Handy Dandy No. 1,* p. 3
salt and pepper to taste
4 eggs

In a large bowl, combine all ingredients except the eggs and mix thoroughly. Beat the eggs and fold them into salmon mixture. Pour into a casserole (about 1½-quart size) and bake, uncovered, in a 350° oven for 1 hour or longer—until firm in the center.

Ahead of time: Everything except the eggs can be combined and mixed in the morning. Leave covered at room temperature until time to bake, then beat eggs and add as directed.

Tip: Ruth Benson says (and she is right) that this is delicious cold the next day; it also reheats beautifully.

Dorothy Wolpert's Salmon Mousse

[makes about 1 quart]

1 tablespoon unflavored gelatin (1 envelope)
3 tablespoons lemon juice
3 slices onion
½ cup rapidly boiling water
½ cup mayonnaise
½ teaspoon paprika
1 teaspoon dill (or more)
1 (1-pound) can salmon, drained
1 cup heavy cream

Place the gelatin and lemon juice in the container of a blender and let stand for 3 minutes. Add the onion and boiling water and blend 1 minute. Add the mayonnaise, paprika, dill, and salmon (remove some of the salmon skin if you wish) and blend another minute. With blender still running, remove the cover and gradually add the cream. Blend about another 30 seconds. Pour into a large mold (or into individual ones) and refrigerate for 8 to 24 hours. Unmold and serve with *Remoulade Practicality, Handy Dandy No. 10*, p. 9, or *Sour-Cream Dill Sauce, Handy Dandy No. 5*, p. 5.

Ahead of time: This can be made the day before; it must be prepared no later than the morning before serving.

Tip: This makes an exceptionally delicious first course at dinner, served either in the living room or at the dining-room table.

Salmon Steaks with Anchovy Butter and Anchovies

[serves 6]

¼ cup butter	salad oil
1 tablespoon anchovy paste	18 flat anchovies, well
6 fresh salmon steaks	drained and separated
salt and pepper	

Whip or cream the butter and anchovy paste together and set aside. Season the salmon lightly with salt and pepper and place in an oiled baking pan. Sprinkle each steak with oil, then broil to your taste. Remove from broiler, spread with some of the anchovy butter, and garnish each serving with 3 anchovies. Serve at once.

Ahead of time: Anchovy butter will keep for weeks in the refrigerator and for many months in the freezer.

Super-Easy Whole Salmon Baked in Foil

[serves 8 to 12]

1 whole, very fresh salmon
  (6 to 8 pounds)
juice of ½ lemon
salt and pepper
½ cup chopped green
  onions

½ cup grated parmesan
  cheese
½ cup melted butter

for sauce (optional)

½ cup melted butter
½ cup sour cream

½ teaspoon onion salt

Rub the salmon inside and out with lemon juice. Season with salt and pepper. Combine the onions and parmesan and stuff the fish cavity. Place fish on a very large piece of heavy-duty foil. Pour ½ cup melted butter over the fish. Fold up foil around fish and seal well. Place on a large baking sheet. Bake for approximately 1½ hours at 350° (assuming fish is at room temperature). Do not remove foil, but place fish on a platter and serve directly from the foil. There will be an enormous amount of delicious juice to serve with the fish. But you may also want to make a sauce: just whisk the sauce ingredients together over very low heat. Serve separately.

Ahead of time: The salmon can be seasoned, stuffed, and wrapped in foil in the morning and left at room temperature ready to bake. If you plan to serve it cold, bake it the day before and refrigerate overnight.

Tip: This is nice with a sliced-tomato salad and boiled, parsleyed new potatoes. If you prefer, you can puncture the foil from the bottom over a very large warmed platter and let the juices run out, then remove the fish to another platter and pour juices over it before serving. If you serve it cold, try it with *Sour-Cream Dill Sauce, Handy Dandy No. 5*, p. 5.

Sea Bass for Parties

[serves 8; for 16 or 24, double or triple quantities]

salt and pepper	2 tablespoons lemon juice
flour	1 tablespoon minced
4 pounds sea bass fillets	dehydrated onion
1½ cups sour cream	1 tablespoon warm water
1 cup mayonnaise	3 tablespoons chopped
1 teaspoon salt	fresh dill
½ teaspoon pepper	grated parmesan cheese

Lightly season sea bass with salt and pepper, then roll fillets in flour. Shake off excess flour and place fish in a large, shallow casserole (or several casseroles). Make the sauce by combining sour cream, mayonnaise, salt, pepper, lemon juice, soaked dehydrated onion, and dill. Cover fish completely with this sauce. Sprinkle with the grated parmesan and bake, uncovered, at 350° for 30 to 45 minutes, depending on temperature of fish and sauce.

Ahead of time: This can be completely assembled in the early afternoon, covered, and left at room temperature. Or it can be done in the early morning and refrigerated. Bring to room temperature before baking, or bake longer.

Red Snapper with Olives

[serves 4]

1 onion, chopped	4 red snapper fillets
2 tablespoons butter	1 cup pitted green olives or
salt and pepper	small pimento-stuffed
2 cups canned tomatoes,	green olives
mashed	

Place the chopped onion and the butter in a shallow ovenproof casserole (glass or enamel) and season lightly with salt and pepper. Place in a 400° oven and bake for 10 minutes, stirring once or twice. Add the tomatoes and bake an additional 10 minutes. Remove from oven. Season the fish with salt and pepper and add to the casserole. Spoon the tomato-onion mixture over the fish. Return casserole to oven and bake about 15 to 20 minutes, basting once. Scatter the olives over the fish and continue baking for about 5 minutes. Serve hot from the casserole.

Ahead of time: If you plan to serve it cold—it makes a superb cold summer fish dish—it can be made the day before and refrigerated.

Rex Sole Extraordinaire

[serves 4]

4 large rex soles (about ½ pound each) or 8 small ones

salt and pepper

for the sauce

1 cup sour cream
½ cup mayonnaise
1 tablespoon chopped parsley

½ teaspoon salt
¼ teaspoon pepper
½ cup grated cheddar cheese

for the topping

1 cup green seedless grapes (fresh preferably, but canned may be used)

½ cup grated cheddar cheese

Season the fish lightly with salt and pepper and place in a greased shallow casserole. Combine the sauce ingredients and spoon on the fish. Bake uncovered in a 350° oven for 20 to 30 minutes. Remove from oven and sprinkle with the topping ingredients. Return to oven for about 8 minutes. Serve directly from the casserole.

Ahead of time: This can be arranged with sauce on top in the morning and refrigerated until about 1 or 2 hours before cooking. Bake and add topping as in recipe. Should any be left over, it reheats remarkably well the next day, or is good cold.

Swordfish Steaks with Fresh Tomato and Green Onion

[serves 2]

2 swordfish steaks (each
  about ½ pound)
3 tablespoons oil
  salt and pepper

1 large ripe tomato, sliced
2 green onions, chopped
2 tablespoons butter

Roll the swordfish in the oil, season, then place in a shallow casserole. Place under the broiler for about 7 minutes. (Do not turn.) Remove, cover with tomato slices, and top with green onion. Dot with the butter. Turn oven to 400° and bake uncovered for about 10 minutes, basting once. (Time will depend on temperature of the fish and its thickness.) Serve from the casserole with a small spoonful of the pan juices on each portion.

Two Whitefish without Worry

[serves 8]

2 whole large whitefish
  salt and pepper
6 shallots (or ½ onion),
  chopped
2 cloves garlic, mashed, or
  garlic from *Garlic Oil,
  Handy Dandy, No. 1,* p.
  3

4 tablespoons oil
½ cup dry white wine
¼ cup (or more) melted
  butter
¼ cup chopped parsley

Season the fish inside and out with salt and pepper. Combine the shallots or onion and garlic and place in the cavity of each fish. Rub the outside of each fish with the oil and place them in a very large baking pan (glass, enamel, or stainless steel). Pour in the wine. Bake at 400°, basting occasionally, for about 45 minutes. Remove from oven, pour the butter over the fish, sprinkle them with parsley, and serve at once.

Crabmeat on Toast Croutons

[6 modest portions]

6 slices white bread, crusts removed
softened butter
1 (7-ounce) can crabmeat
1 cup grated cheddar cheese
½ teaspoon salt
¼ teaspoon pepper
1 teaspoon Worcestershire sauce
2 tablespoons chopped green onion
3 tablespoons mayonnaise

To make croutons, butter the bread generously and toast it by baking it for approximately 10 minutes in the upper part of a 425° oven. Combine the crabmeat with the remaining ingredients. Divide onto the buttered side of the toast slices. Place under the broiler to brown, then serve.

Ahead of time: The crabmeat mixture can be made the day before and refrigerated. These can be completely assembled in the morning; cover with plastic wrap and leave at room temperature until time to broil.

Lobster Delicious

[serves about 6]

4 frozen lobster tails (about 6 to 8 ounces each)
1 medium-sized onion, chopped
¼ cup butter
⅓ cup dry vermouth
⅓ cup sour cream
⅓ cup mayonnaise
salt and pepper
chopped fresh parsley

Defrost the lobster and remove from shells. Cut in large bite-sized pieces. Sauté the onion in the butter until tender, then add the lobster and stir over medium heat for a minute or two. Add the vermouth, reduce heat, and cook another minute. Add the sour cream, mayonnaise, salt, and pepper and simmer for another 2 minutes, covered. Do not overcook. Taste for seasoning and serve very hot, garnished with chopped parsley.

Ahead ot time: This can be assembled in the morning or the day before. Refrigerate but bring to room temperature about 2 hours before serving. Reheat over low heat, stirring all the time. Do not overcook. Or, easier, reheat in a 300° oven in a covered casserole, stirring once or twice.

Hot Shrimp Heaven

[serves about 10 as a main course]

5 pounds extra large (or jumbo) shrimp, raw and in the shells

for the brine

6 quarts water	4 garlic cloves, cut in half,
¾ cup salt (yes!)	or garlic from *Garlic Oil,*
3 large onions, sliced or	*Handy Dandy, No. 1,* p.
coarsely chopped	3
2 teaspoons cayenne pepper	1 cup sliced celery
2 lemons, squeezed and	½ teaspoon thyme
then dropped in brine	½ teaspoon tarragon
1 cup vinegar	1 teaspoon basil
1½ cups dry white wine	3 bay leaves

Devein the shrimp but leave them in the shells. Refrigerate. To make the brine, combine all other ingredients in a large pot and bring to a boil. Simmer for 30 to 45 minutes, then strain and return the liquid to the pot. Shortly before serving bring liquid to a boil. Add the shrimp and bring to a gentle simmer. Simmer about 3 minutes and turn off heat. Let shrimp stand in pot for another 3 minutes. Drain and serve hot with individual bowls of melted butter and lemon wedges.

Ahead of time: The brine can be prepared the day before and strained. In an enamel or stainless-steel pot, it can stand overnight at room temperature. The shrimp can be cleaned in the morning and refrigerated. Heat the strained brine, add the shrimp and cook, and you will have achieved *Hot Shrimp Heaven* without any last-minute effort.

Tip: Not for a formal occasion. This calls for a relaxed atmosphere and plenty of paper napkins, since guests must peel their own shrimp at table.

Easiest

Halibut, Unharried

[serves about 4]

4 halibut steaks (or 2 extra-
  large ones)
salt and pepper
½ cup finely sliced celery
½ cup chopped green onion

1 (8-ounce) can tomato
  sauce
2 tablespoons butter
  (optional)

Season the halibut steaks with salt and pepper and place in a greased casserole. Top halibut steaks with celery and onion and spoon the tomato sauce over vegetables. Dot with butter (if desired) and bake in a 400° oven for about 20 to 25 minutes (if fish is at room temperature).

Ahead of time: The celery and onion can be chopped and refrigerated the day before or in the morning.

Tip: Excellent cold, which makes a fine summer lunch.

No Trouble Halibut

[serves 6 to 10]

1 whole piece of fresh
  halibut (3 to 5 pounds)
salt and pepper
1 (10¾-ounce) can
  condensed tomato soup

1 cup heavy cream
1 large onion, chopped
1 to 1½ cups chopped
  celery

Season the halibut with salt and pepper and place in a large shallow casserole. Combine the remaining ingredients and pour over the fish. Bake at 350° for 30 minutes; reduce heat to 275° and bake about another 30 to 45 minutes (depending on the size, temperature, and shape of the fish). Serve from the casserole, spooning sauce over each portion.

Ahead of time: The soup mixture can be assembled the day before or in the morning and refrigerated.

Tip: Delicious with buttered noodles and asparagus.

Salmon Steaks Simple

[serves 4]

4 salmon steaks	1 (13-ounce) can shrimp
salt and pepper	bisque (Crosse &
½ cup finely chopped celery·	Blackwell)
½ cup chopped onion	2 or 3 tablespoons sherry

Season the salmon with salt and pepper and place in a lightly greased casserole. Top each steak with chopped celery and onion. Combine the bisque and sherry and spoon over the salmon. Bake uncovered in a 400° oven for 25 to 30 minutes. Serve directly from casserole.

Ahead of time: The celery and onion can be chopped the day before or in the morning. Fish, soup, and sherry can be assembled in the early afternoon, covered, and left at room temperature until time to bake.

Tip: Excellent with something like *Corn Casserole*, p. 187-88, and *Bean Sprout and Tomato Salad* p. 210.

Jane Ilfeld's Delicious but Easy Baked Salmon

[serves 8 to 10]

4- to 5-pound piece of fresh
    salmon, boned, then
    cut into two long fillets
salt and pepper
juice of 1 lemon

¼ cup melted butter
2 (10¾-ounce) cans
    condensed tomato soup
½ teaspoon basil

Season the salmon with salt and pepper and place in a large shallow casserole. Cover with the lemon juice and melted butter, then top with the tomato soup and basil. Bake uncovered at 325° for about 1 hour; baste, then continue baking another 30 minutes.

Ahead of time: The fish with its sauce-seasoning can be assembled several hours before time to bake.

Tip: When salmon is in season, this makes an ideal party dish, with no muss or fuss.

Red Snapper Fillets Baked with Handy Dandy No. 5

[serves about 4]

4 medium-large red snapper
    fillets
salt and pepper
flour

1½ cups *Sour Cream Dill*
    Sauce, Handy Dandy No.
    5, p. 5
chopped chives or green
    onions

Season fish and lightly dust with flour. Shake off excess. Place in a single layer in a lightly greased shallow casserole. Cover with the sauce to mask fish completely. Bake at 400° about 20 minutes or so (longer if cold). Garnish with a sprinkling of chopped chives or green onions.

Ahead of time: This can be completely assembled in the morning and refrigerated. Bring to room temperature an hour or so before baking.

Sole Veronica Super-Easy

[serves 4]

fillets of sole (about 2
    pounds)
salt and pepper

1 (13-ounce) can Crosse &
    Blackwell shrimp bisque
1½ cups seedless grapes

Season fish with salt and pepper. Place in a shallow casserole and cover with the bisque. Bake at 400° for 15 to 20 minutes, baste, then add grapes and bake about another 5 minutes.

Satellite Swordfish

[serves 4]

2 pounds swordfish
salt and pepper

2 cups Italian tomato sauce
    (bought or homemade);
    see, *Tomato Sauces A and
    B, Handy Dandy No. 11
    and No. 12,* p. 10

Season the fish lightly. Place in a casserole and cover with the sauce. Bake at 375° for about 25 minutes, then just serve with rice or pasta of your choice.

Tunafish Emergency Goodies

[serves 2 to 4]

1 (7-ounce) can tunafish, drained
1 cup finely chopped celery
¼ cup finely chopped green onion
2 tablespoons lemon juice

½ cup (generous) mayonnaise
salt and pepper (as needed—taste)
sliced cheddar cheese

Combine all ingredients except cheese. Place in a casserole (or in individual ones) and cover with cheese slices. Bake in a 400° oven for about 20 minutes, or until very hot and bubbly.

Ahead of time: This can be assembled either the day before or in the morning and refrigerated. Bring to room temperature an hour or so before baking.

Tip: Excellent either as a first course or a luncheon or light supper dish.

Baked Smoked Whitefish Presto

1 or more smoked whitefish (preferably each weighing 2 pounds or more)

parsley

Place fish on an ovenproof platter and cover tightly with aluminum foil. Bake at 350° for about 30 minutes—only until very hot. Remove from foil and surround with parsley. Serve with *Sour-Cream Dill Sauce, Handy Dandy No. 5, p. 5,* or *Remoulade Practicality, Handy Dandy No. 10, p. 9.*

Tip: Not only super-simple but absolutely delicious. I like to serve this with hot boiled new potatoes and either a fresh green cooked vegetable or a splendid salad.

Elegant Crabmeat

[serves 4 as a main course; 8 as an appetizer]

1 pound of the best fresh crabmeat you can find salt to taste (crabmeat varies in salt content)	1 tablespoon lemon juice ½ teaspoon (about) cracked black pepper ¾ cup softened butter

Combine the crabmeat with the salt, lemon juice, and black pepper and place in a casserole. Spread the softened butter over the entire top. Just before serving, place in a 450° oven for about 5 to 7 minutes—just until sizzling hot. Do not overcook.

Tip: If you are unable to buy fresh crabmeat you might try this with fine-quality canned. I find frozen crabmeat completely tasteless.

Crabmeat Casseroles

[serves about 4]

2 (7-ounce) cans crabmeat ½ green pepper, chopped 6 green onions, chopped 1 cup finely chopped celery 1¼ cups mayonnaise 4 tablespoons lemon juice salt and pepper to taste 1 garlic clove, mashed, or garlic from *Garlic Oil, Handy Dandy, No. 1,* p. 3	½ teaspoon Worcestershire sauce few drops Tabasco grated parmesan cheese

Combine all ingredients except cheese in a bowl and mix. Divide into individual casseroles. Sprinkle with grated cheese. Bake at 400° for 20 to 30 minutes. (If you like, brown the tops under a broiler.)

Ahead of time: Everything can be assembled the day before. Refrigerate until 2 hours before time to bake.

Herbed and Baked Scallops

[serves 2 or 3]

⅔ cup dry bread crumbs
   (commercial are okay)
1 teaspoon salt
½ teaspoon pepper
1 teaspoon basil
1 teaspoon dill weed

1 teaspoon sugar
1 pound scallops, well
   drained and dried on
   paper towels
¼ cup melted butter
¼ cup oil

Combine crumbs, seasonings, and herbs in a bowl. Combine butter and oil in another bowl. Dip scallops in butter-oil mixture, roll in crumb mixture, and place in a single layer on a foil-lined baking pan. Bake at 425° for 12 to 15 minutes. Don't overcook. Serve with lemon wedges and a sauce—for example, *Russian Dressing, Handy Dandy No. 8, p. 8; Sour-Cream Dill Sauce, Handy Dandy No. 5, p. 5; Red Cocktail Sauce, Handy Dandy No. 9, p. 8 or Remoulade Practicality, Handy Dandy No. 10, p. 9.*

Ahead of time: The crumb mixture can be combined several days ahead; keep it tightly covered.

Tip: Marvelous extra-easy appetizers.

Shrimp in Foil

[4 small servings or 2 generous ones]

¼ cup soft butter
¼ cup chopped parsley
1 garlic clove, mashed, or
   garlic from *Garlic Oil,*
   Handy Dandy, No. 1, p.
   3

½ teaspoon salt
¼ teaspoon pepper
1 pound raw shrimp,
   deveined and shells
   removed

Cream together all ingredients except shrimp. Divide the shrimp into four portions and place them in the center of four foil squares (10 by 10 inches). Divide the flavored butter over the shrimp and bring foil up and around each packet, sealing well. Just before serving place packets on a baking pan and bake in a 400° oven for 15 minutes. Serve hot in the foil packets.

Ahead of time: These can be readied in the morning and refrigerated; bring them to room temperature before baking.

Tip: These can be a lovely first course, or a main course for lunch or, in larger portions, a simple dinner.

5/POULTRY

Easy

Roast Chicken with Tamale Stuffing

[serves 4 to 6]

1 large roasting chicken (5
   to 7 pounds)
salt and pepper
*Garlic Oil, Handy Dandy
   No. 1, p. 3*

ground cumin
1 onion, coarsely chopped
¾ cup dry red wine

for stuffing

2 (15-ounce) cans tamales,
   cut in ½-inch pieces
1 cup whole-kernel corn
2 tablespoons chopped
   onion

1 teaspoon chili powder
1 teaspoon ground cumin
salt and pepper to taste

Combine the stuffing ingredients. Season the inside of the chicken with salt and pepper, then fill with the stuffing. (Put any extra stuffing in a casserole and cover with foil; put in oven with chicken when chicken has cooked about 40 minutes.) Season the outside of the chicken with salt, pepper, *Garlic Oil*, and cumin. Place the onion on the bottom of a heavy Dutch oven, then put chicken on top with the giblets around it. Cover and roast in a 450° oven for 1 hour and 10 minutes. (Do not uncover during this time.) Remove from oven and add the wine, cover, and return to oven for another 10 to 15 minutes.

Ahead of time: The stuffing can be made the day before and kept refrigerated. The entire chicken can be prepared and cooked in the morning, but shorten the first roasting period to about 1 hour. Leave at room temperature. To finish, add wine, reheat, covered, in a 350° oven about 30 minutes. Heat extra stuffing for the same time (longer if cold).

Exotic Indonesian-Style Chicken

[serves 4 generously]

2 chickens, split into halves   salt and pepper
   (each about 2 pounds)

for the baste-marinade

¼ cup vinegar
   rind and juice of 1 lemon
1 teaspoon mashed garlic
   and 2 tablespoons oil
   from *Garlic Oil, Handy
   Dandy No. 1,* p. 3
1 tablespoon minced
   dehydrated onion
1 teaspoon celery seeds

1 teaspoon oregano
2 tablespoons soy sauce
1 teaspoon salt
2 teaspoons A-1 sauce
2 tablespoons curry powder
2 dashes Tabasco
⅓ cup Dijon-style mustard
⅓ cup honey

Prepare the baste-marinade: Combine all ingredients in a saucepan, then stir and heat, but only until sauce boils. Remove from heat and cool to room temperature. Season the chickens lightly with salt and pepper. Place them in a baking pan skin side down. Cover with about one third of the marinade. Bake at 350° for about 40 minutes. Add a little water to pan if marinade starts to burn. Turn chickens over (now skin side should be up) and spoon on one third more of the marinade. Bake an additional 30 to 45 minutes, or until chickens are tender. Add more marinade and water as needed during the cooking. If there is any leftover marinade, gently reheat it and serve as a sauce to be passed at table.

Ahead of time: This can be prepared the day before or in the morning; underbake a little, cover and refrigerate. Bring to room temperature, then reheat (and baste) in a 350° oven. This freezes very well; defrost and bring to room temperature, then proceed with the heating and basting.

Tip: For a little extra elegance, garnish with chopped pistachios.

Eileen Taylor's
Chicken-Broccoli Casserole

[serves about 10]

3 packages frozen broccoli
   spears, defrosted and
   well drained (I do not
   cook them)
8 large chicken breasts,
   cooked, skinned,
   boned, and cut in large
   pieces
2 (6-ounce) cans sliced
   mushrooms, partially
   drained; reserve 1
   tablespoon liquid
2 (10¾-ounce) cans
   condensed cream of
   mushroom soup

1 cup mayonnaise
1½ tablespoons lemon juice
½ teaspoon curry powder
1 package Pepperidge Farm
   stuffing mix (about 4
   cups dry)
water and butter to
   prepare stuffing
½ cup grated parmesan
   cheese

Arrange the broccoli in a large shallow casserole. Place the chicken pieces over the broccoli. Combine the soup, mushrooms and 1 tablespoon mushroom liquid, mayonnaise, lemon juice, and curry powder (I do not bother heating this). Spread over the chicken. Prepare the stuffing according to package instruction and spread on top. Cover with the grated parmesan. Bake, uncovered, at 350° for about 30 minutes (until very hot and browned).

Ahead of time: This can be assembled in the morning or the day before. Refrigerate until about 1 hour before time to begin baking and allow 1 hour or more to heat the casserole (because of the refrigeration).

Tip: Perfect for a buffet lunch or dinner, and the recipe can easily be doubled and assembled in two casseroles.

Chicken Marsala

[serves 8]

8 boned and skinned
  chicken breasts
salt and pepper
flour
¼ cup butter
½ pound fresh mushrooms,
  sliced

2 tablespoons butter
¾ cup rich chicken stock
½ cup dry marsala
¼ cup grated parmesan
  cheese

Season the chicken breasts with salt and pepper, then dust with flour. Sauté gently in the ¼ cup butter in a large skillet until lightly browned. *Do not overcook.* Reserve the butter in the skillet. Place chicken breasts in an ovenproof casserole large enough to hold them in one layer without crowding. Sauté the mushrooms in the skillet, adding the 2 tablespoons additional butter. Season mushrooms with salt and pepper, then spoon them onto the chicken. Add the stock and marsala to the skillet and reduce a little, then spoon over the mushrooms and chicken. Sprinkle the parmesan on top. Cover lightly with plastic wrap and leave at room temperature until ready to bake. Then remove the plastic wrap, cover tightly with foil, and bake in a 350° oven for 25 minutes. Remove the foil and bake an additional 5 to 10 minutes.

Ahead of time: This can be prepared up to the point of the baking either in the morning or the day before and refrigerated. Bring to room temperature (remove from refrigerator about 2 hours before baking), and bake as directed.

Roast Turkey in Foil with Supermarket Stuffing

[serves 10 to 16]

1 (12-pound) turkey
salt and pepper
Supermarket Stuffing, p.
  92
2 onions, sliced
¼ cup *Garlic Oil, Handy
  No. 1*, p. 3.

½ cup soy sauce
4 tablespoons flour (for
  thickening the gravy)
2 to 4 tablespoons sweet
  marsala or sweet sherry

seasoning mixture:

2 teaspoons salt
½ teaspoon pepper

½ teaspoon thyme
½ teaspoon basil

Season turkey inside with salt and pepper. Stuff with *Supermarket Stuffing*. Skewer openings. Prepare two very long overlapping strips of heavy-duty foil, place the sliced onions in the center, then place stuffed turkey on top of the onions. Surround with the giblets and neck. Combine the *Garlic Oil* and soy sauce and paint the entire turkey, pouring whatever remains over top of turkey. Combine the ingredients of the seasoning mixture and sprinkle entire turkey with this. Now wrap the whole thing up in the foil, folding and pressing where needed to seal. Place foil-wrapped bird on a rack in a large roasting pan. Roast in a 450° oven for 3 hours, then reduce heat to 325° and roast 1 more hour. Remove from oven and poke holes in the bottom of the foil to release all the juices into a saucepan. Unwrap the bird and add the onions to the juices. Lift bird to an ovenproof platter and return to oven for 30 minutes (or longer if needed) to brown and finish cooking.

To make the gravy: Remove the fat from juices and discard all but 4 tablespoonfuls. Put this fat in a saucepan with the 4 tablespoons flour, blend over low heat, and gradually add the juices (there should be almost 4 cups; if not, add chicken stock). Bring to a boil, stirring constantly. Reduce heat to a simmer and cook for 5 minutes. Add the marsala or sherry and cook 1 minute.

Ahead of time: The *Supermarket Stuffing* can be made the day before, but keep it refrigerated. The turkey can be stuffed and wrapped in foil in the morning, but not more than 3 hours before you plan to begin cooking it.

Tip: Try the *Garlic Oil*–soy combination and the seasoning mixture on separate turkey thighs or, for those who like only white meat, on a whole turkey breast.

Supermarket Stuffing

[enough for a 12-pound turkey, plus some]

1 onion, chopped	½ cup hot water
¾ pound butter	½ teaspoon poultry
2 packages (6½ ounces	seasoning
each) Mrs. Cubbison's	
"ready to use" melba	
toasted dressing	

Sauté the onion in the butter over moderate heat for several minutes. Add the remaining ingredients and toss. Turn heat as low as possible, cover, and leave for about 2 minutes. Remove from heat but leave cover on until stuffing has cooled; then refrigerate.

Ahead of time: This is best made early in the morning or the day before. The stuffing can also be frozen.

Tip: Any stuffing that doesn't fit into the bird, place in a casserole and sprinkle with chicken broth (about ⅔ cup for each 3 or 4 cups of stuffing). Cover lightly with foil and bake at 325° to 350° for about 45 minutes.

One-Baste Duckling with Pineapple, Bananas, and Apricots

[serves 4 generously]

2 ducklings
salt and pepper
3 onions
2 celery stalks, cut in pieces
fresh pineapple slices
banana chunks, brushed
    with lemon juice
canned apricot halves

butter (melted)
2 cups duck stock (made
    from necks, giblets, and
    wing tips, cooked in
    canned chicken broth)
2 tablespoons cornstarch
¼ cup cold water

Remove excess fat from the ducklings. Season with salt and pepper. Stuff each with 1 onion (cut in quarters) and some celery. Place them in a roasting pan with the third onion (coarsely chopped or sliced). Prick the skin of the ducklings, then cover tightly with pan cover or with heavy foil. Roast at 350° for 1½ hours. Do not uncover during this time. Remove pan from oven, discard onion, and remove all fat. (Save fat for some other purpose, such as making pâtés.) Increase oven heat to 425°, baste ducklings with juices, then return to oven, uncovered, and roast about another 30 minutes. Place each of the three fruits in separate foil pans and brush generously with melted butter. Remove ducklings to a large ovenproof platter. Discard any additional fat that may have accumulated. Strain the duck stock and add to the pan. Bring to a boil and scrape all the good brown bits into the stock. Dissolve the cornstarch in the cold water and add, stirring constantly. Reduce heat and simmer a few minutes. Meanwhile, place the fruits in the oven and heat (about 5 to 10 minutes in the 425° oven should be ample).

Arrange the fruit around the ducklings. Bring to table and carve, or cut in halves or quarters with a poultry scissors. Serve each guest some of each fruit, along with a generous portion of the sauce.

Ahead of time: The ducklings can be cooked early in the day, the sauce prepared, and the fruits arranged in the foil pans with butter over them. Keep at room temperature, loosely covered. Shortly before serving, reheat ducklings in a 400° oven about 15 to 20 minutes. Reheat sauce, heat fruit, and serve as directed.

One-Baste Duckling with Peaches, Plums, and Grapes

2 ducklings
salt and pepper
3 onions
2 celery stalks, cut in pieces
2 cups duck stock (made from necks, giblets, and wing tips cooked in canned chicken broth)
grated rind of 1 orange

juice of 2 oranges
grated rind of 1 lemon
juice of ½ lemon
2 tablespoons cornstarch
⅓ cup currant jelly
2 fresh peaches, peeled and quartered
4 fresh plums, quartered
1 cup seedless grapes

Remove excess fat from ducklings. Season with salt and pepper. Stuff each with a quartered onion and some celery. Place in roasting pan with the third onion (coarsely chopped or sliced). Prick skin of ducklings, then cover tightly with pan cover or with heavy foil. Roast at 350° for 1½ hours. Do not uncover during this time. Remove pan from oven, discard onion and remove all fat. (Save for another purpose.) Increase oven heat to 425° and baste ducklings with juices, then return to oven uncovered and roast about another 30 minutes. Remove ducklings to a large ovenproof platter. Discard any additional fat that accumulated. Add strained duck stock to pan, and bring to a boil, scraping the good brown bits into the stock. Strain into a saucepan. Dissolve cornstarch in the orange and lemon juices and add the grated rinds. Add this to the stock, add the currant jelly, and bring to a boil, stirring constantly. Reduce heat and simmer 2 minutes. Add the peaches, plums, and grapes and cook 1 or 2 minutes, just long enough to heat the fruit. Remove all fruit from sauce and arrange around the ducklings for serving. Give each guest some of the fruit plus generous spoonfuls of the sauce over both duckling and fruit.

Ahead of time: As in the preceding recipe the ducklings can be cooked early in the day; the sauce can also be prepared, except for the fruit. Shortly before serving reheat ducklings and sauce, add the fruit to the sauce, and proceed as above.

Magda Loeb's Game Hens with Port-Cherry Sauce

[serves 6 or 12]

1 cup chicken broth
1 cup dry white wine
¼ cup madeira

6 game hens
salt and pepper
¼ cup melted butter

for the sauce

2 cups port wine
¼ teaspoon powdered cloves
⅛ teaspoon each: nutmeg, allspice, thyme
grated rind of 1 orange
juice of 1 orange
½ cup red-currant jelly

1 to 2 cups pitted Bing cherries (canned or frozen are fine)
2 tablespoons cornstarch, dissolved in ½ cup cold water

Combine the chicken broth, white wine, and madeira and simmer, uncovered, 30 minutes, then remove from heat. Meanwhile, make the sauce: combine port, cloves and other spices, orange rind and juice, and cook uncovered until reduced to about half (about 20 to 30 minutes). Stir in the jelly and cherries, then thicken to taste with the dissolved cornstarch (stirring while adding) over moderate heat. Season the game hens with salt and pepper and place in a roasting pan. Pour melted butter over each. Broil briefly (about 5 minutes), then pour sauce over and cover with foil. Bake at 350° for 1 hour or until tender. Baste after about 45 minutes. If you want the hens brown, bake uncovered for about 15 minutes at the end. Add any juices left from cooking the hens to the sauce. To the brown bits in the pan add a little chicken stock to deglaze the pan and add to the sauce.

Place game hens on a heated platter and serve sauce in a separate bowl. Serve each guest 1 hen (or half a hen) and spoon sauce over.

Ahead of time: Game hens can be cooked in the morning, left at room temperature, then reheated at 275° for about 35 minutes. The sauce can be made several days ahead, kept refrigerated, then reheated gently before serving.

Game Hens in Individual Cookers

[serves 4]

4 game hens	*Garlic Oil, Handy Dandy*
salt and pepper	*No. 1*, p. 3
3 tablespoons minced	1½ cups chopped celery
dehydrated onion,	½ to ¾ cup marsala (dry or
soaked in ½ cup warm	sweet)
water	

Use individual casseroles with covers (Pyrex are fine or, if you can find them, the ceramic ones shaped like small chickens). Remove necks and giblets from the game hens and reserve. Season insides of hens generously with salt and pepper. Place a little onion and celery inside each. Oil the casseroles, then place some of the remaining onion and celery in the bottom of each, seasoning them with salt and pepper. Coat the outside of the hens generously with *Garlic Oil* and season outsides with salt and pepper. Place hens in casseroles and surround with the necks and giblets, seasoning these also. Spoon a tiny bit more *Garlic Oil* over each hen in the casserole. Cover, then place in a 500° oven. Reduce heat at once to 450° and roast 30 to 45 minutes. Remove from oven and add about 2 to 3 tablespoons marsala to each casserole. Turn hens upside down, cover, and leave at room temperature until about 30 minutes before serving time. Then return hens to their upright position. Cover casseroles and roast again at 450° for 30 minutes. Bring to table and give each guest a casserole and a serving spoon to help lift hens to dinner plates and to spoon out the exquisite sauce that has formed in the bottom of each casserole, and two hot-pad-holders to avoid burning hands.

Ahead of time: Start these in the late morning or early afternoon, as you want the hens to stand awhile upside down in their casseroles.

Tip: Serve the game hens with any favorite rice, noodle, or potato dish, or, easier, with an excellent French bread that can be used to soak up those superb juices.

Chicken Parmesan Modernity

[serves 8]

2 eggs
1 tablespoon water
¾ cup dry bread crumbs
¾ cup grated parmesan
   cheese
2 teaspoons salt
½ teaspoon pepper
½ teaspoon oregano
½ teaspoon basil

8 chicken breasts, skin
   removed
½ cup butter (or more as
   needed)
½ pound grated cheese
   (mozzarella or swiss or
   jack)
2 cups tomato sauce
   (canned)

Beat the eggs slightly with the water. Combine bread crumbs, parmesan, salt, and herbs. Dip the chicken breasts in the eggs, then coat thoroughly with crumb mixture. Sauté chicken in the butter over moderate heat—just brown each side. Be careful not to burn it. Place chicken pieces side by side in a large shallow casserole. Divide the cheese over the pieces of chicken. Spoon the tomato sauce on top. Cover tightly with foil. Bake for 40 minutes at 350°. Remove foil, baste, then bake about another 10 minutes.

Ahead of time: This can be done the day before or in the morning. Bake only 30 minutes with the foil. Cool, cover, and refrigerate. To serve, bring to room temperature, bake covered at 350° for 30 minutes, then uncover and bake 10 minutes.

Honey, Orange, Ginger Chicken

[serves 4 or more]

2 large frying chickens, split
  in halves
¼ cup oil
¾ cup soy sauce
1 cup honey
  grated rind of 2 oranges
  juice of 2 oranges

1 tablespoon grated or
  finely minced fresh
  ginger
1 clove garlic, mashed, or,
  better, garlic from *Garlic
  Oil, Handy Dandy, No. 1,*
  p. 3

Place the chicken halves, skin side down, in a baking pan. Combine the remaining ingredients and pour ¾ of this mixture over chicken. Bake 1 hour at 350°, basting occasionally. Turn chicken, pour remaining sauce over it, and bake approximately ½ hour longer, basting several times.

Ahead of time: This can be done in the morning. Leave at room temperature, covered with plastic wrap. Reheat in a 350° oven, basting frequently.

Tip: Excellent served cold the next day.

Chicken Breasts with a Magic Mushroom Sauce

[serves 10]

10 chicken breasts, boned
   and skinned
   salt and pepper
   flour
½ cup butter
½ pound fresh mushrooms,
   finely chopped (or put
   through a meat grinder)
3 green onions, chopped

4 tablespoons flour
  pinch of tarragon
2 cups rich chicken stock
  (or canned chicken
  broth)
1 cup sour cream
3 tablespoons cognac
  chopped parsley

Season the chicken breasts with salt and pepper. Roll them in flour, then sauté gently in a large skillet in ¼ cup of the butter. Remove from pan. Add the remaining ¼ cup butter to the skillet and sauté the mushrooms over high heat for about 2 minutes. Add the green onions, sprinkle with the flour, and stir until blended. Add the tarragon and the chicken stock and stir constantly until sauce comes to a boil. Remove from heat. Place chicken breasts and sauce in a casserole. Cover and bake at 325° for 30 minutes. Remove from oven. Remove chicken from casserole and place in a heatproof serving dish. Add the sour cream and cognac to the sauce and heat, stirring, until sauce is hot but not boiling. Pour the sauce over the chicken. Put the dish in the oven just long enough to make certain chicken and sauce are very hot. Garnish with chopped parsley.

Ahead of time: This lends itself beautifully to preparation either the day before or in the morning. Reheat, covered, in the oven. It freezes beautifully. Defrost, then reheat gently in the oven.

A Rosemary-Marsala Chicken Marvel

[serves 4 to 6]

1 large roasting chicken (6 to 7 pounds)
salt and pepper
Garlic Oil, see *Handy Dandy No. 1*, p. 3
1 to 2 tablespoons rosemary (yes, tablespoons!)

2 onions, coarsely chopped or sliced
⅓ cup dry marsala (or sherry or madeira)

Have the chicken at room temperature. Season inside and out, including giblets, with salt, pepper, *Garlic Oil*, and rosemary. Put one chopped onion inside the chicken, and the other on the bottom of a Dutch oven or roasting pan or heavy casserole. Place the chicken on top of the onion. Arrange giblets around chicken. Cover as tightly as possible and roast without lifting the cover in a 450° oven for 1 hour and 10 minutes. Remove from oven, un-cover, add the wine, then cover again. Reduce oven temperature to 350° and cook about 10 to 15 minutes. Bring to table in the roasting pan and remove the cover in front of your guests. Place the chicken on a platter to carve. Spoon over each portion some of the rich sauce that has created itself.

Ahead of time: This can be done in the morning, all but the fi-nal roasting. Leave chicken out at room temperature. Just before serving, put it in a 350° oven and roast only until very hot (about 15 to 20 minutes).

Divine Chicken Divan

[serves 4]

4 chicken breasts, cooked
1 (10¾-ounce) can
    condensed cream of
    chicken soup
¾ cup mayonnaise
⅓ cup chicken stock
1 tablespoon lemon juice

salt and pepper to taste
2 tablespoons madeira
1 package frozen broccoli,
    defrosted
about 1 or 2 tablespoons
    grated parmesan cheese
    for each chicken breast

Place chicken breasts in a casserole with a little water and salt and pepper, cover, and bake them at 350° for 45 minutes to 1 hour; cool in broth overnight in the refrigerator. Remove skin and bones from breasts, but leave as whole as possible. Combine soup, mayonnaise, stock, lemon juice, salt and pepper, and ma-deira. Place the broccoli in an ovenproof casserole and spoon on about one third of the sauce. Place chicken on top of this, then spoon on the remaining sauce. Sprinkle each breast with parme-san. Bake, uncovered, at 350° for 30 to 40 minutes—until hot and lightly browned.

Ahead of time: This can be completely assembled the day be-fore or in the morning and kept refrigerated. Either bring to room temperature before baking or increase the baking time.

Broiled Chicken Halves with Rosemary

[serves 6 generously]

3 broiler-fryer chickens,
split in halves (ask
poultryman to remove
the backbones and wing
tips, to use later for
stock)

oil
salt and pepper
2 tablespoons dried
rosemary, or 4
tablespoons fresh
1 cup dry white wine

Rub the chickens generously with oil and season well with salt and pepper, then with plenty of rosemary. Broil slowly, first with skin side down, then with skin side up (total time should be about 40 to 50 minutes). Place chickens on a platter and keep warm in a low oven. Remove excess fat from the pan, add the wine, and place pan over high heat, scraping to get all the good brown bits. Pour over chicken and serve.

Tip: If this is part of a rather large dinner, the chickens can be quartered after broiling; each guest then is given a quarter rather than a half, and theoretically (with no second helpings) this would serve 12. The chicken is excellent served cold the next day. And do try serving this with *Ported Prunes, Handy Dandy No. 22*, p. 18.

Simplicity Turkey Creole

[serves 4 to 6]

1 onion, chopped
1 green pepper, chopped
4 tablespoons olive oil or
butter
½ cup stock or gravy
1½ cups canned tomatoes

½ can tomato paste (3
ounces)
salt and pepper
¼ teaspoon oregano
3 cups diced cooked turkey

Sauté the onion and green pepper in the oil or butter until tender. Add stock or gravy, tomatoes, tomato paste, salt, pepper, and oregano. Simmer slowly, uncovered, for 45 minutes or so. Add the turkey and heat slowly. Serve with brown or white rice.

Ahead of time: This can be done in the morning or the day before and can be frozen. In all cases, reheat slowly, stirring gently.

Turkey-Mushroom Hurry-Curry

[serves 12]

2 large onions, chopped
¾ cup butter
2½ pounds fresh mushrooms, sliced
juice of ½ lemon
salt and pepper to taste
4 cups thickened rich turkey gravy (lacking this, thicken some bouillon or other stock)

3 teaspoons curry powder (or more)
6 to 8 cups diced cooked turkey

CHOICES OF CONDIMENTS

sliced bananas
chopped green onions
chopped green pepper
toasted coconut
plumped raisins
chutney

crisp bacon, crumbled
chopped candied ginger
chopped toasted almonds
chopped hard-cooked eggs

Sauté the onions in the butter until tender and lightly browned. Add the mushrooms and cook a few more minutes. Add the lemon juice, salt, and pepper, stir, cover, and cook 1 minute. Add the remaining ingredients, stir, and simmer uncovered for about 5 minutes. Taste for seasoning. Serve with brown or white rice and some or all of the condiments.

Ahead of time: The curry can be prepared the day before and refrigerated. Reheat gently before serving. The condiments (except the sliced bananas) can also be prepared the day before; store them, covered, in the refrigerator, but bring to room temperature before serving. The curry can be frozen; defrost, then reheat, and serve as directed.

Teriyaki Broiled Game Hens

[serves 4 to 8]

4 game hens   *Teriyaki Basic Marinade,*
                               Handy Dandy, No. 3, p.
                               4

Split the game hens through the breast but *not* through the backbone. Remove wing tips. Flatten hens and put a skewer through them to keep them flat. Place them in a broiler pan, skin side down. Spoon some of the marinade over them. Broil, not too close to broiler unit, until well browned, basting occasionally with additional marinade. Add water to the pan if the liquid begins to dry out and burn. Turn hens skin side up and continue to broil, basting occasionally, until browned (and even slightly charred) and tender. If hens brown too much, finish by roasting in a 375° oven rather than broiling.

Tip: These are lovely served with *Gingered Rice,* p. 167, and *Ported Prunes, Handy Dandy No. 22,* p. 18.

A Facile Solution for Fancy Game Hens

[serves 6]

6 game hens   ½ cup dry red wine
  salt and pepper   1 package dried onion
1 (1-pound) jar grape jelly   soup
⅔ cup orange juice

Season the hens lightly with salt and pepper and place breast side down in a roasting pan. Combine the remaining ingredients and pour the mixture over the hens. Roast at 350° for 45 minutes. Turn hens breast side up and baste. Roast another 40 or more minutes, or until tender. If the sauce thickens too much during the roasting, add a little more wine or orange juice.

Ahead of time: These can be done in the morning, but don't overcook. Before serving, roast in a 350° oven about another 30 minutes. Can be frozen, but they are so easily done, why bother? Freezing is worthwhile, however, for any leftovers.

Tip: This recipe can be doubled or even tripled without any trouble, making it a perfect entrée for a big party—assuming you have more than one oven.

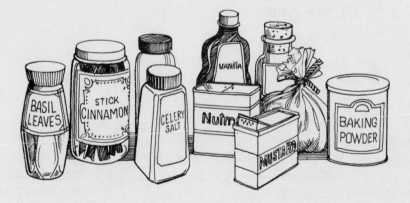

Walter Horn's Easily Prepared Chicken Wings

[serves 4 to 6]

18 to 20 chicken wings
    pepper
⅓ cup soy sauce
⅓ cup sherry

⅔ cup water
2 or 3 green onions,
    chopped (optional)

Season the wings with pepper and place in a glass or ceramic casserole in one layer, top sides down. Combine the soy sauce, sherry, and water and pour over them. Broil about 15 to 20 minutes, basting occasionally, then turn and continue broiling and basting for about another 20 minutes. Sprinkle with green onions if desired and bring to the table in the casserole. Serve with Chinese boiled thin noodles.

Tip: These are extraordinary and superb. Better plan to have at least 3 to 4 per person. I like the sherry in this marinade to be on the sweet side, but that is a matter of taste.

No-Work Chicken-Sauerkraut Casserole

[serves 4]

8 chicken legs or thighs
    salt and pepper

1 pound sauerkraut, rinsed
    and well-drained
2 cups tomato purée

Place half of the sauerkraut and half of the tomato purée in a casserole. Season the chicken pieces, then add them to the casserole. Top with the remaining sauerkraut and tomato purée. Cover and bake at 350° for 1½ to 2 hours. Serve hot from the casserole along with boiled new potatoes or buttered noodles.

Ahead of time: This can be prepared in the morning or the day before. And it freezes too.

Suzanne Mellinkoff's Roasted Chicken

[serves 2 to 4]

1 cut-up fryer chicken
(about 2½ pounds)
salt and pepper
1 or 2 garlic cloves, minced,
or garlic from *Garlic Oil,
Handy Dandy*, No. 1, p.
3

1 teaspoon rosemary
juice of 1 small lemon
½ cup cream sherry or
madeira (not dry
sherry)
4 tablespoons butter or
margarine, melted

Season the chicken and place in a baking pan. Pour all the other ingredients over the chicken and roast at 350° for about 45 minutes to 1 hour, basting about every 15 or 20 minutes. Serve hot with a little of the sauce that forms in the pan.

Ahead of time: This is best eaten at once; however, it is delicious cold the next day.

Joanne Weiner's Stewed Chicken

[serves 6 to 8]

2 roasting chickens or large
fryers (about 3½
pounds each), cut in
pieces
a little garlic from *Garlic
Oil, Handy Dandy No. 1*,
p. 3
salt and pepper

3 celery stalks, cut in 1½-
inch pieces
3 carrots, cut in 1½-inch
pieces
1 onion, chopped
1 cup canned tomatoes
(mostly all tomatoes
and little juice)

Season the chicken with garlic, salt, and pepper, and layer the pieces in a casserole or Dutch oven, placing heavier pieces on the bottom. Sprinkle the vegetables with salt and pepper and spread over chicken, then add the tomatoes. Cover tightly and simmer on top of stove for about 2½ hours or until tender. Or, if preferred, bake in a casserole in a 325° oven.

Ahead of time: This can be prepared the day before or in the morning and it freezes beautifully. Reheat gently before serving.

Tip: Joanne suggests serving this with boiled noodles and homemade croutons, the latter made by sautéing bread cubes in butter.

Chicken Thighs Teriyaki

[serves 8 to 16]

16 chicken thighs

2 cups *Teriyaki Basic Marinade, Handy Dandy No. 3, p. 4*

Place the chicken thighs in a large shallow casserole, skin side down. Pour the marinade over chicken and bake at 350° for 35 minutes. Turn chicken skin side up and bake about another 35 minutes.

Ahead of time: The chicken can be cooked in the morning, then reheated just before serving.

Chicken Breasts with Parmesan and Mustard

[serves about 8]

1 cup dry bread crumbs
1 cup grated parmesan cheese
1¼ teaspoons salt
½ teaspoon pepper
1 cup melted butter

1 teaspoon Worcestershire sauce
4 teaspoons Dijon-style mustard
8 chicken breasts, skinned

Combine the crumbs, parmesan, salt, and pepper. In another bowl combine the butter, Worcestershire sauce, and mustard. Dip each chicken breast in the butter mixture, then roll in the crumb mixture. Place in a shallow casserole (or in a pan lined with foil) in one layer. Spoon any remaining butter mixture over the chicken. Bake uncovered in a 350° oven for 1 hour, baste, and then bake about ½ hour longer.

Ahead of time: This can be prepared in the morning. Bake for 45 minutes, then leave at room temperature just lightly covered. Before serving, place in a 350° oven (uncovered) and bake another 45 to 50 minutes, basting once if time permits.

Tip: This can also be made with boned chicken breasts. Reduce baking time somewhat for the boned version.

Baked Chicken Casseroles Super-Simple

[serves 6]

3 cups diced chicken
1½ cups chopped celery
2 teaspoons dehydrated
   minced onion soaked in
   ¼ cup water
2 cups shredded cheddar
   cheese

1 tablespoon lemon juice
¾ to 1 cup mayonnaise
salt and pepper, only if
   needed
¾ cup toasted slivered
   almonds

Combine all ingredients except the almonds and divide into 6 individual casseroles (or put in one large shallow casserole). Top with almonds. Bake at 350° for 15 to 20 minutes.

Ahead of time: This can be assembled the day before or in the morning.

Fast and Easy Chicken Curry

[serves about 4]

1 (10¾-ounce) can
   condensed cream of
   mushroom soup
⅔ cup chicken stock
1 teaspoon dehydrated
   minced onion

½ teaspoon paprika
1½ to 2 teaspoons curry
   powder
4 cups diced cooked
   chicken
salt and pepper as needed

Combine the soup, stock, onion, paprika, and curry powder in a saucepan. Stir over moderate heat until sauce boils, reduce heat, and simmer for a few minutes. Add the chicken and heat slowly for 5 to 10 minutes, stirring occasionally. And that's it! Serve with rice and any condiments you like.

Ahead of time: This can be made the day before or in the morning; and it freezes too.

Chicken Simplicity

[serves 6 to 8]

2 chickens, quartered
1 cup well-seasoned *French Dressing, Handy Dandy No. 7,* p. 7

1 cup apricot jam
1 package dried onion soup

Place the chicken quarters skin side down in a large roasting pan. Combine the remaining ingredients and spoon over chickens. Bake uncovered at 350° for 1 hour; turn chicken over, baste, and bake another 45 minutes, or until tender and browned.

Ahead of time: This can be prepared the day before or in the morning; if so, undercook a little. This can also be frozen; again, undercook. Defrost before reheating.

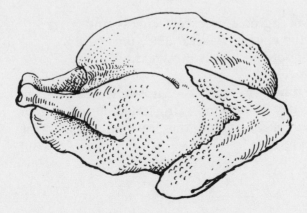

Baked Chicken Super Deluxe and Easy

[serves 2 to 4]

1 chicken, split in half,
seasoned with salt and
pepper
1 cup sour cream

1 (10¾-ounce) can
condensed cream of
mushroom soup
½ cup sherry

Place chicken halves skin side down in a casserole large enough
so pieces do not touch. Combine the remaining ingredients and
pour over chicken. Bake at 325°, uncovered, for 45 minutes.
Turn chicken skin side up and bake an additional 45 minutes.

Ahead of time: This can be prepared in the morning, but be
sure to undercook the chicken; reheat in a 325° oven before serving.

Tip: Try serving this garnished with chopped toasted almonds.

Time-Saver Chicken Casserole

[serves 4 to 6]

3 or 4 cups cubed cooked
chicken
1 (10¾-ounce) can
condensed cream of
celery soup
1 cup sliced celery

1 teaspoon minced
dehydrated onion
½ cup grated parmesan
cheese

Combine all ingredients except cheese and place in a casserole.
Top with the cheese. Bake at 350°, uncovered, for 30 to 40 minutes—until hot and lightly browned.

Ahead of time: This can be completely assembled in the morning or the day before and refrigerated. Bring to room temperature before baking. And this freezes; defrost, then bake as
directed in recipe.

Easy-Does-It Baked Chicken

[serves 5 to 10]

10 pieces chicken (breasts,
  thighs, or drumsticks)
  salt and pepper
2 (10¾-ounce) cans
  condensed cream of
  mushroom soup

1 package dried onion soup
½ cup dry sherry

Combine the mushroom soup, dried onion soup, and sherry and mix thoroughly. Arrange the chicken pieces in one layer in a large shallow pan or casserole, or use two pans—do not layer the chicken. Season very lightly with salt and pepper (not too much salt). Spoon sauce over all pieces of chicken. Place uncovered in a 300° oven and bake for 2 to 3 hours, or until chicken is tender and thoroughly browned.

Ahead of time: This can be assembled the day before or in the morning, then refrigerated until about an hour or so before baking.

Joanne Weiner's Way with Barbecued Turkey Thighs

[serves about 6]

3 turkey thighs (about 5
  pounds total weight)
1 onion
  salt and pepper

½ cup Open Pit Barbecue
  Sauce, or any favorite
  sauce, commercial or
  homemade

Place the turkey thighs and the onion in a roasting pan. Season with salt and pepper, then pour the sauce over turkey and onion. Cover and bake 1½ to 2 hours in a 350° oven; reduce heat to 300°, add water or stock if necessary, cover again, and bake about ½ hour longer, or until tender.

Ahead of time: This can be done in the morning; it reheats well.

Tip: I have had good luck using turkey wings or breast of turkey in this recipe.

Another Turkey Curry without Worry

[serves 5]

2 onions, chopped
½ cup butter
⅓ cup flour
4 cups chicken stock or
  turkey stock
¼ teaspoon thyme

1 tablespoon chopped fresh
  parsley
1 tablespoon curry powder
  (or more)
5 cups diced cooked turkey

Sauté the onions in the butter until golden. Add the flour, then the stock, and cook over low heat, stirring, until bubbling. Add the thyme, parsley, and curry powder and heat for 5 minutes. Add the turkey and cook over lowest heat for 10 minutes. Serve with your favorite kind of rice and any or all of the condiments listed for *Turkey-Mushroom Hurry-Curry*, p. 102.

Ahead of time: This can be prepared the day before or in the morning. Refrigerate. Reheat gently before serving. And it can be frozen. Defrost, then reheat and serve as directed.

I'm Easy Duckling with a Cranberry-Onion Sauce

[serves 2 to 4]

1 duckling, quartered
  salt and pepper
1 clove garlic, mashed, or,
  better, garlic from *Garlic
  Oil, Handy Dandy No. 1*,
  p. 3

1 package dried onion soup
2 tablespoons flour (scant)
1 (1-pound) can whole-
  berry cranberry sauce
½ cup dry red wine

Remove any excess skin and as much fat as possible from the duckling. Season duckling with salt and pepper and place in a large roasting pan. Combine the remaining ingredients, mix well, then spoon over duckling pieces. Roast, covered, at 300° for 2½ hours without basting or removing cover. Drain or spoon off all the fat from the sauce in the pan and transfer the sauce to a saucepan. Leave duckling in roasting pan. Shortly before serving place duckling in a 350° oven, uncovered, and roast about 20 minutes. Reheat sauce over low heat.

Ahead of time: This can be prepared in the morning or the day before. If done in the morning, leave duckling at room temperature, covered, then reheat as directed. If the day before, refrigerate until several hours before serving, then bring to room temperature and proceed as directed.

Lazy-Day Ducklings

[serves 4 to 8]

1 package dried onion soup
1 (10¾-ounce) can
    condensed cream of
    celery soup

½ cup dry sherry
2 tablespoons soy sauce
2 ducklings

Mix the soups, sherry, and soy sauce together. Place the ducklings in a large roasting pan. Cover ducklings inside and outside with the soup mixture. Cover tightly with a double covering of foil (or use heavy-duty foil). Place in a 250° oven for 3 hours (don't peek). Remove from oven. Place ducklings on an oven-proof platter. Pour the accumulated juices and fat into a large saucepan. Skim off all the fat (save it for making pâtés, sautéing chicken livers, etc.). Place the ducklings, uncovered, in a 425° oven and roast for 20 to 30 minutes, until well browned and crisp. While ducklings are crisping reheat the sauce.

Ahead of time: The ducklings can be given the initial 3-hour roasting in the morning. Leave them at room temperature, lightly covered, until time to finish roasting them.

Tip: Serve with *Ported Prunes, Handy Dandy No. 22*, p. 18.

6/MEAT

Boeuf à la Bourguignonne Effortless but Sumptuous

[serves 10 to 12]

5 tablespoons flour
5 tablespoons soy sauce
1 (6-ounce) can tomato
   paste
5 pounds stew beef (after
   trimming), cut in 2-inch
   cubes
4 large onions, sliced
2 carrots, sliced
1 cup celery, sliced

2 cloves garlic, mashed, or,
   better, 2 teaspoons garlic
   from Garlic Oil, Handy
   Dandy No. 1, p. 3
1 teaspoon black pepper
¾ teaspoon salt
¾ teaspoon thyme
2 bay leaves
2½ cups dry red wine

CHOICE OF VEGETABLES

fresh celery slices, cooked
   crisp-tender
freshly cooked carrots
fresh peas, cooked (or
   frozen or canned)
small onions, boiled
fresh mushrooms, sautéed

fresh zucchini, sliced and
   briefly sautéed
fresh green beans, cooked
   crisp-tender
small new potatoes,
   boiled

Combine the flour and soy sauce, then stir in the tomato paste. Place the beef in a very large casserole, add the flour-soy-tomato paste mixture and stir until beef cubes are coated. Add all the remaining ingredients and stir again. Cover tightly, place in a 450° oven, and bake 15 minutes, then reduce temperature to 250° and continue cooking until meat is just tender—about 2 to 3 hours. Taste for seasoning about an hour before it is done; add more salt and pepper if needed. Remove from oven and serve with one or more of the suggested vegetables. Either add them to the stew and heat briefly, or serve them at the side on the dinner plates.

Ahead of time: This is best when done a day ahead, then reheated slowly in a 275° or 300° oven. But it can be made several days ahead and it freezes well.

Tip: The quantities indicated are for a large party or for those who want to divide the results for freezing; however, do not hesitate to cut the recipe in half.

Beef Fondue with Sauces

½ pound per person beef tenderloin trimmed of all fat, skin, and gristle, then cut into ¾-inch or 1-inch cubes
salt and pepper at table
good-quality cooking oil
(Wesson oil, peanut oil, etc., but not olive oil), enough to half-fill chafing dish or fondue pan. An ordinary fondue pan takes a little more than 1 quart.

Sauces

1 *Garlic mayonnaise:* Combine 1 cup mayonnaise with some garlic from *Garlic Oil, Handy Dandy No. 1,* p. 3, and cover for at least several hours or overnight.

2 *Curry mayonnaise:* Combine 1 cup mayonnaise with 1 or more tablespoons curry powder (or more) and 2 teaspoons lemon juice; cover for at least several hours.

3 *Horseradish sauce:* Combine 2 tablespoons prepared horseradish and 1 cup whipped cream or sour cream with 1 teaspoon salt and 1 tablespoon vinegar or lemon juice. Chill.

4 *Tomato ketchup* (Heinz): Pour straight out of the bottle into an attractive dish.

5 *Dijon-style mustard:* Spoon right out of the jar into a small dish.

6 *Sour-Cream Dill Sauce, Handy Dandy No. 5,* p. 5.

7 *Russian Dressing, Handy Dandy No. 8,* p. 8.

8 *In the Manner of Hollandaise, Handy Dandy No. 4,* p. 5.

To serve: Assemble all the sauces in separate bowls and place on a large tray (or trays). Arrange meat cubes and two forks per guest (one for cooking and one for eating) on individual fondue plates or regular dinner plates. Place oil in fondue pan or chafing dish and heat. Your guests must do the rest themselves.

Ahead of time: All the sauces that require preparation (except *In the Manner of Hollandaise*) can be done completely the day before and kept refrigerated until shortly before serving. The mock hollandaise can be assembled the day before but must be gently heated immediately before serving.

Tip: This is a lovely do-it-yourself dinner; you can simplify it even more by providing only three or four sauces. I suggest serving with the fondue the *Raw Vegetable Platter*, p. 211, and *Parmesan French Toast*, p. 230.

Prime Ribs of Beef Deluxe but Simple, with Onions, Carrots, and Potatoes

[serves 8 to 12]

prime rib beef roast,
  about 8 to 10 pounds
salt and pepper
2 or 3 large baking
  potatoes, peeled, then
  quartered lengthwise
16 to 20 small carrots, peeled

2 or 3 large onions,
  quartered (or medium-
  sized ones, halved)
⅓ cup oil
2 (10½-ounce) cans
  condensed beef bouillon

Season the meat with salt and pepper and place it in a very large baking pan (I use one about 17 by 12 by 2 inches). Dip the vegetables in the oil and arrange them around the meat. Pour any surplus oil over the vegetables, then season with salt and pepper. Roast uncovered at 325° for 45 minutes. Add the bouillon to the pan and roast about another 45 minutes or longer (until meat reaches desired doneness), basting once or twice. Remove the roast to a carving board and while it rests return the pan with the vegetables to the oven for another 15 minutes. Arrange the vegetables in a serving dish and pour the sauce over them. Carve the roast and serve along with an assortment of vegetables, plus a little sauce over each portion.

Ahead of time: Vegetables can be peeled in the morning. Place them in a bowl of cold water until time to cook.

Steaks Sensational

[serves 6]

6 beef tenderloin steaks, about 1½ to 1¾ inches thick salt and pepper olive oil	6 small slices of *Pâté Pangloss*, p. 24, or good-quality canned pâté de foie gras

for the sauce:

1 tablespoon chopped shallots (see *Shallots Preserved, Handy Dandy No. 2*, p. 3) 2 tablespoons corn or peanut oil	2 tablespoons flour 1 cup dry red wine 1 cup canned beef bouillon (condensed) ¼ cup ketchup (Heinz) ¼ cup Dijon-style mustard

Prepare the sauce first. Sauté the shallots in the 2 tablespoons oil for 1 or 2 minutes. Add the flour and cook over low heat for another few minutes, then gradually add the wine and bouillon, stirring constantly, until mixture boils. Simmer a minute or so, then add ketchup and mustard and simmer another minute. Remove from heat and set aside. When almost ready to serve, season the steaks with salt and pepper and sauté them to the desired doneness in a heavy skillet in some olive oil. Remove steaks to a heated platter, pour off and discard any oil left in skillet, and pour in the prepared sauce. Heat, scraping up any delicious brown bits. Place the pâté slices on top of the steaks and pour the sauce around (not on) the meat.

Ahead of time: The sauce can be prepared the day before or in the morning.

Tip: For an extra delicious touch, add 2 tablespoons of madeira to the sauce just before pouring it around the steaks.

Walter Horn's Steak Diable Surpris

[serves about 6]

1 "first-cut" blade-cut chuck steak, 2¼ inches thick (It is important for taste and tenderness to get the "first" cut of the chuck; make friends with your butcher.)	2 tablespoons olive oil salt and pepper
2 tablespoons soy sauce	1 cup dry red wine
1 tablespoon dry mustard	1 tablespoon tomato paste (or tomato ketchup)
2 slices bacon, diced (optional)	1 tablespoon dry mustard
1 onion, chopped	¼ teaspoon paprika
1 small garlic clove, mashed, or garlic from *Garlic Oil, Handy Dandy No. 1,* p. 3	1 cup rich beef bouillon
	1 cup chopped parsley
	3 green onions, chopped

Make a paste of the soy sauce and 1 tablespoon dry mustard and rub the steak with it on both sides. Sauté the bacon (if used), the onion, and garlic in the olive oil (gently) until soft. Move onions to side of skillet, add the steak, and brown it on both sides. Do this slowly over moderate heat for 5 to 8 minutes on each side, seasoning it well with salt and pepper. Add the wine, tomato paste or ketchup, 1 tablespoon dry mustard, paprika, and bouillon. Cover and simmer gently for about 5 to 10 minutes (turning if necessary) to desired state of doneness, but don't cook too long—this steak should be served rare or medium-rare. Add the parsley and green onions to the sauce. Remove the meat to a cutting board and put the sauce in a bowl. Carve the meat in thin slices and serve with some of the sauce.

Tip: This fascinating and delicious recipe is truly a surprise— even to the devil—because it transforms a very inexpensive cut of meat into a royal dish. If desired, the sauce can be lightly thickened by adding some *beurre manié* gradually to it while it is simmering. (*Beurre manié* is merely equal quantities of soft or melted butter and flour mixed together; in this case I would use approximately 2 tablespoons butter mixed with 2 tablespoons of flour.)

Sue Grotstein's Chilly Night Chili

[serves 4 to 6]

3 tablespoons vegetable oil (approximate)
2 medium onions, coarsely chopped
2 medium green peppers, chopped in bite-sized pieces
6 to 8 celery stalks, sliced in rather thick pieces
1½ to 2 pounds ground round or chuck beef

salt and pepper to taste
2½ to 4 tablespoons chili powder (more or less, according to taste)
2 (10¾-ounce) cans condensed tomato soup
2 (15-ounce) cans red kidney beans, drained

Heat the oil in a large pot. Add the onions, green peppers, and celery and stir-fry over medium-high heat for about 5 minutes. Remove vegetables from pot. Put the beef in the same pot with salt and pepper to taste. (Option: A teaspoon or so of the chili powder can be added at this point to bring out flavor.) Brown the beef, then return the vegetables to the pot. Add the soup and beans. Stir, add the chili powder, and mix well. Cook over medium heat for 20 to 30 minutes so that flavors blend and mixture is heated through.

Ahead of time: This improves with age. It can be made several days in advance and kept refrigerated, and it freezes beautifully.

Tip: Sue recommends bringing the chili powder to the table so that guests can add more if they like: "This is the way to satisfy those whose motto is 'Some like it hot!' or 'Spice is the variety of life.' " She suggests this chile for a simple and hearty lunch or dinner to be completed with a crisp green salad, heated French or sourdough bread or rolls, and to wash it down, icy cold beer for the adults, cold milk for the kids.

Green Peppers Filled with Meat Loaf
[serves 8]

8 large green peppers
1 (1-pound) can whole
    tomatoes

1 (8-ounce) can tomato
    sauce

for meat-loaf mixture

1½ pounds lean ground beef
1½ teaspoons salt
¼ teaspoon pepper
1 teaspoon dry mustard
1 small onion, grated or
    finely chopped

½ cup dry bread crumbs
¾ cup tomato juice
¼ cup ketchup (Heinz)
¼ teaspoon oregano
2 eggs, slightly beaten

Slice tops off the green peppers and remove seeds. Chop the tops fine and add to the meat-loaf ingredients. Mix those together well. Fill the peppers with the mixture and place them in a shallow casserole. Mash the canned tomatoes with hands (or in a blender), combine with the tomato sauce, and pour around peppers. Bake at 450° for 10 minutes; reduce temperature to 350° and bake about 40 minutes more.

Ahead of time: These can be prepared several days ahead and kept refrigerated; reheat in the oven before serving. These can also be frozen.

Individual Lamb Roasts, Indonesian Style

[serves 4 to 6]

12 to 18 French rib lamb
    chops (ask butcher to
    leave each 3 or 4 chops
    joined together)

for the marinade

¼ cup vinegar	2 bay leaves
rind and juice of 1 lemon	2 tablespoons soy sauce
1 garlic clove, mashed, or	1 teaspoon salt
garlic from *Garlic Oil,*	2 teaspoons A-1 sauce
Handy Dandy, No. 1, p.	2 tablespoons curry powder
3	2 dashes Tabasco sauce
1 tablespoon dehydrated	⅓ cup Dijon-style mustard
minced onion	⅓ cup honey
1 teaspoon celery seeds	⅔ cup oil
1 teaspoon oregano	

Prepare the marinade by combining all ingredients except the oil in a saucepan. Stir and heat until boiling. Remove from heat, then beat in oil. Cool to room temperature. Place the lamb chops in a large pan with fat sides down. Spoon on marinade and leave at room temperature at least 4 hours; they can be left 8 hours. To cook: drain the marinade from the lamb and reserve. Place the chops in a roasting pan, fat sides up. Roast at 450° for about 20 to 30 minutes, basting once or twice with the reserved marinade. Cooking time will depend on temperature of lamb when you begin, and how well cooked you like it. Try to have it at room temperature before cooking.

Ahead of time: This marinade will keep a month or longer in the refrigerator.

Tip: Fresh or canned pear halves filled with chutney make a divine accompaniment for these unusual lamb roasts.

Rack of Lamb, Persillé— a Prescription for Praise

[serves 4 to 6]

1 cup dry bread crumbs
1 teaspoon mashed garlic and 1 tablespoon oil from *Garlic Oil, Handy Dandy No. 1*, p. 3
¼ cup melted butter
½ cup chopped parsley

½ teaspoon salt
2 (6-rib) racks of lamb, well trimmed of almost all fat; bone ends trimmed of fat and gristle
salt and pepper

Combine bread crumbs, garlic, oil, melted butter, parsley, and salt; mix well and set aside. Season the lamb with salt and pepper and place in a roasting pan fat side up. Roast at 450° for 15 minutes. Remove from oven and pat crumb mixture on the fat sides of the lamb racks. Baste with the drippings in the pan to make the crumb topping adhere. Return to oven and roast another 10 minutes or longer (depending on how well done you want the lamb). Remove to a serving platter or cutting board; carve at the table and serve.

Ahead of time: The crumb mixture can be made days ahead of time and kept refrigerated. Bring to room temperature before using. The mixture can be made in large quantities, divided, and frozen for use later.

Tip: If you like, add a little bouillon to the drippings and crumbs in the roasting pan; bring to a boil and pour around, but not on, the racks of lamb. Ask your butcher to prepare the racks for carving: Have the chine bone and practically all the fat removed and for easier carving have the places marked for carving the ribs. Have the meat scraped about 1½ inches from the ends of the bones. During roasting time you can wrap the exposed tips with foil to avoid burning, though I have not found this necessary.

Leg of Lamb with Mustard, Rosemary, and Garlic

[serves 6 to 8]

1 leg of lamb (5 or 6
   pounds)
salt and pepper
1 onion, chopped
2 or 3 carrots, chopped
½ cup Dijon-style mustard
1 teaspoon rosemary
2 teaspoons mashed garlic
   from *Garlic Oil, Handy
   Dandy No. 1*, p. 3

1 tablespoon soy sauce
4 tablespoons salad oil
½ cup dry red wine
2 cups beef bouillon
   (canned is okay)

Remove all fat and all skin from the outside of the lamb. Season with salt and pepper. Chop the onion and carrots and place on the bottom of a roasting pan. Combine the mustard, rosemary, mashed garlic, and soy sauce, then beat in the salad oil. Spread this mixture on the underside of the leg, then place the leg on top of the carrots and onion underside down and spread the top and sides of the lamb with the remaining mixture. Roast without basting at 350° for 1½ to 2 hours, depending on the weight of the meat and how well done you like it. Before serving, remove the lamb to a warm platter and discard any grease in the roasting pan. Deglaze the pan with the red wine and bouillon. Serve some of this sauce with each slice of lamb.

Ahead of time: The lamb can be completely coated with the mustard mixture in the morning and left (covered) at room temperature until time to roast it.

Tip: You may want to thicken the sauce lightly; if so, dissolve 2 tablespoons cornstarch in about ⅓ cup cold water and add this to the sauce, stirring constantly until sauce comes to a boil. Reduce heat and simmer gently for 1 minute.

Leg of Lamb Guadalajara

[serves 6 to 8]

for the sauce:

3 teaspoons mashed garlic from *Garlic Oil, Handy Dandy No. 1*, p. 3

1 onion, chopped

2 tablespoons butter

1 (1-pound) can tomatoes

1 tablespoon oregano

1 tablespoon ground cumin

½ teaspoon salt

1 teaspoon chili powder

2 tablespoons oil

1 leg of lamb (5 or 6 pounds)
  salt and pepper

1½ cups beef bouillon (canned is fine)

Make the sauce: Sauté the garlic and onion in the butter for about 3 minutes, then add the tomatoes, mashing them up well. Simmer for about 5 minutes, then add the oregano, cumin, salt, and chili powder. Simmer covered for 15 minutes; uncover and simmer an additional 5 minutes. Place in blender a little at a time, along with the oil, and spin until smooth. Let cool.

Remove all fat and all skin from the outside of the lamb. Season with salt and pepper. Cover lamb with the cooled sauce and roast at 350° to desired doneness (about 1½ to 2 hours); do not baste. Add the beef bouillon to the pan after the lamb is about half cooked.

Ahead of time: The sauce can be made the day before or in the morning. It can be frozen; defrost and use as directed.

Tip: This is excellent served with *Corn and Green Chile Casserole*, p. 152, or with *Rice, Green-Chile, Jack-Cheese, and Sour-Cream Heaven*, p. 168.

Easier

Top Sirloin Steak Baked Really Sensational

[serves 8 to 10]

1 top sirloin steak, cut 3½ inches thick (about 5 pounds)
⅓ cup oil and 1 teaspoon mashed garlic from *Garlic Oil, Handy Dandy, No. 1*, p. 3
salt and pepper
1 onion, thinly sliced
½ green pepper, thinly sliced

1 cup ketchup (Heinz)
½ cup chili sauce (Heinz)
1 lemon, thinly sliced (leave the peel, just remove seeds)
1 tablespoon Worcestershire sauce
½ cup dry red wine

Place the steak in a roasting pan and roll it in the oil. Season with salt and pepper. Place the garlic and onion on top, then cover with the green pepper, ketchup, and chili sauce. Top with the lemon slices and then add the Worcestershire sauce. Roast in a 500° oven for 25 minutes. Add the wine to the pan and baste, then return to oven, reducing heat to 300°. Roast about another 20 to 30 minutes, basting once or twice if you have time. To serve, place the steak on a cutting board. Pour the sauce (which has made itself during the roasting) into a separate bowl (reheat if necessary). Carve the steak at the table, serving some sauce with each portion.

Ahead of time: The onion and green pepper can be sliced the day before or in the morning; keep in tightly sealed plastic bags in the refrigerator.

Tip: Serve this with *New Potatoes, Easily Roasted*, p. 190.

A Glorious Mexican Beef Stew—Made from Leftover Roast Beef

[serves about 4]

1 clove garlic, mashed, or use garlic from *Garlic Oil, Handy Dandy No. 1,* p. 3
1 large onion, chopped
¼ cup oil or bacon fat
4 cups cubed leftover beef (roast, stewed, or braised)

1½ teaspoons ground cumin
1 (7-ounce) can green chile salsa
salt and pepper to taste

Sauté the garlic and onion in the oil or bacon fat for about 2 minutes. Add the beef and cook over high heat, stirring, for another 2 minutes. Add the remaining ingredients and simmer over lowest heat for about 1 hour or longer.

Ahead of time: This can be done the day before and kept refrigerated. Reheat gently before serving. This can be frozen.

Tip: Excellent served with rice, tortillas, or refried beans—or all three.

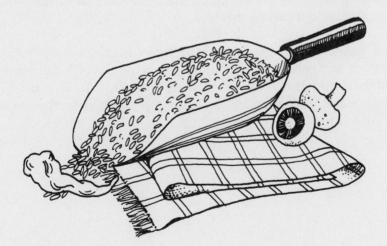

Beef and Onion Simplicity Goulash

[serves 6 to 8]

3 pounds boneless beef (chuck or other), cut in 2-inch cubes

2 cloves garlic, mashed, or garlic from *Garlic Oil, Handy Dandy, No. 1,* p. 3

4 or 5 onions, sliced

4 teaspoons salt

1 teaspoon pepper

2½ teaspoons paprika

1 (1-pound) can of tomatoes, drained (save juice for another purpose)

2 bay leaves

4 tablespoons soft butter mixed with 4 tablespoons flour (optional)

Combine the beef, garlic, onions, salt, pepper, and paprika in a large casserole or Dutch oven. Crush the tomatoes with your hands and place on top, along with the bay leaves. Cover tightly and place in a 225° oven for 8 to 9 hours (overnight). Remove from oven, discard bay leaves, let cool, and, if time permits, chill. Remove congealed fat. If you wish to thicken the gravy, heat the casserole on top of the stove and stir in the butter-flour mixture until desired thickness is achieved. Serve with any starch—pasta or potatoes or rice.

Ahead of time: This can be made three days ahead of time and refrigerated; and it can be frozen.

Tip: If this is served the same evening, it isn't necessary to re-frigerate it and reheat it, although I think the flavor is enhanced and the calories from the fat reduced by doing so. If you omit the thickening, serve the goulash in soup bowls with spoons in addition to forks and knives.

Joe's Special: Beef and Spinach San Francisco Style

[serves 4 to 6]

1 onion, finely chopped	1 package frozen chopped
¼ pound fresh mushrooms, sliced (optional; or use canned ones)	spinach, defrosted and drained
4 tablespoons butter	salt and pepper to taste
1 pound lean ground beef	6 beaten eggs

Sauté the onion and mushrooms in a large skillet in the butter until lightly browned, then add the beef and cook until it has browned. Stir in the spinach and season. Cook for 1 minute. Pour in the eggs and stir until lightly set. Turn over once and cook another minute or so. Serve very hot with sour dough bread and butter.

Ahead of time: The mixture can be made in the morning or early afternoon. Leave it in the skillet at room temperature, then reheat and add the eggs.

Veal Chops Marsala

[serves 6]

6 veal chops, cut 1¼ inches thick	3 tablespoons butter
salt and pepper	½ cup dry marsala
flour	1 cup chicken stock
	grated parmesan cheese

Season the chops with salt and pepper. Dust with flour. Sauté in a skillet in the butter until lightly browned, then place the chops in a shallow casserole that will hold them in a single layer. Add the marsala and chicken stock to the skillet and bring to a boil. Pour over chops. Cover casserole with foil and bake at 325° for about 35 minutes. Uncover and sprinkle chops with grated parmesan. Bake an additional 10 minutes, uncovered.

Ahead of time: This can be prepared the day before or in the morning. If doing it ahead, bake chops only 30 minutes, cool, then cover and refrigerate. Bring to room temperature several hours before serving, then bake covered for 15 minutes at 325°. Proceed as above.

Idyllic Lamb Stew

[serves about 6]

2 large onions, coarsely chopped or sliced	¼ teaspoon oregano
4 tablespoons butter	¼ teaspoon rosemary
2½ to 3 pounds lean lamb stew meat, cut in pieces	2 tablespoons chopped parsley (see *"Frosted" Herbs, Handy Dandy No. 6, p. 6*
salt and pepper to taste	1 cup heavy cream or sour cream
5 tablespoons flour	
2 cups canned tomatoes	
¼ teaspoon basil	

Sauté the onions in the butter in a skillet for 2 minutes. Add the lamb pieces and sear briefly (stirring) for 2 minutes. Sprinkle flour over meat and stir, then add the tomatoes, basil, oregano, and rosemary and cook, stirring constantly, until mixture comes to a boil. Add salt and pepper. Cover, turn heat down to lowest simmer, and cook slowly for about 2 hours or until lamb is tender. Add the parsley and cream, stir well, and keep warm over low heat.

Ahead of time: This can be prepared the day before or in the morning. Refrigerate, then reheat. It freezes well too.

Tip: This is one of my most favorite dishes; it is superb with fresh peas and freshly cooked noodles.

Leftover Lamb Delicious

[serves about 4]

2 medium onions, sliced
3 tablespoons butter or oil
3 celery stalks, sliced
1 green pepper, sliced
4 cups diced cooked lamb
1 (6-ounce) can tomato
    paste

1 (10½-ounce) can
    condensed beef bouillon
¼ cup water
salt and pepper to taste

Sauté the onions in the butter or oil in a skillet for a few minutes, then add the celery and green pepper and cook a few minutes more. Add the lamb and sauté 3 minutes. Add the remaining ingredients and simmer for about 1 hour over lowest heat, covered. Uncover and simmer another 30 minutes. Serve hot with rice or noodles.

Ahead of time: This can be prepared as much as several days ahead and refrigerated, or it can be frozen. I like it better when reheated the next day—like so many things, it improves with a 24-hour wait.

Pork Chops Teriyaki

[serves 6]

¼ cup ketchup (Heinz)
1½ cups *Teriyaki Basic*
    Marinade, Handy Dandy
    No. 3, p. 4

6 lean pork chops, cut 1¼
    to 1½ inches thick

Combine the ketchup with the *Teriyaki Marinade.* Place the pork chops in a glass or enamel dish and pour the mixture over them. Cover with plastic wrap and marinate at least several hours (turning once) or overnight in the refrigerator. To cook: Remove chops from marinade; reserve it. Broil the chops about 2 minutes on each side. Finish by baking at 400° for about 20 minutes, basting occasionally with some of the extra marinade.

Ahead of time: As indicated in the recipe, you can marinate and refrigerate the pork chops the night before.

Mary Cullins' Barbecued Spareribs

[serves about 8]

6 to 8 pounds lean pork
    spareribs
salt and pepper
1½ cups pineapple juice
¼ cup brown sugar

½ cup chili sauce
1 cup tomato ketchup
1 teaspoon celery seeds
1 onion, finely chopped
dash of nutmeg

Season the ribs with salt and pepper. Place in a large roasting pan and bake (covered) at 450° for 30 minutes, turning once or twice. Remove accumulated fat. Combine the remaining ingredients and pour over ribs. Reduce heat to 300° and bake, basting and turning occasionally for about another hour, or until tender. (This final baking can be done partly covered and partly uncovered.)

Ahead of time: These can be done the day before, or in the morning. They can be frozen; defrost and reheat.

Chinese-Style Spareribs

[serves 6 to 8]

5 pounds lean pork
    spareribs
salt and pepper

2 cups *Teriyaki Basic*
    Marinade, Handy Dandy
    No. 3, p. 4
½ cup ketchup (Heinz)

Season the spareribs lightly with salt and pepper. Place them in a large roasting pan and bake them (covered) at 450°, for 30 minutes, turning once. Remove all accumulated fat. Combine the *Teriyaki Marinade* with the ketchup and pour half the mixture over the ribs. Reduce oven heat to 300° and bake for 40 minutes, uncovered. Turn the ribs, pour on the rest of the sauce and bake an additional 40 minutes or so (until tender), basting occasionally. Remove any excess fat and serve hot or at room temperature.

Ahead of time: These can be prepared several days ahead. Refrigerate. To serve, reheat, lightly covered, in a 300° oven. These can be frozen too.

══════Easiest

Stripper Roast

[serves 12 to 14]

1 (8-pound) New York
   sirloin stripper roast
   (the cut from which
   New York sirloin steaks
   are taken)

salt and pepper

Season the meat with salt and pepper and make sure it is at
room temperature before cooking begins. Roast at 450° for 15
minutes. Reduce oven to 325° and cook about 30 to 35 minutes
longer (for medium-rare). Timing cannot be exact because much
depends upon the exact configuration of the meat and its temperature when roasting begins. It is not necessary to baste this
roast. If possible, let meat rest for 10 to 15 minutes before carving.

Tip: For a holiday buffet, cook this in the morning. Cover, leave
at room temperature, and carve without reheating. It has a superb flavor served at room temperature. And try varying the
taste by adding garlic and herbs to the pre-roasting seasoning.

Unruffled Cross Ribs

[serves 6 or fewer, depending on appetites]

6 large meaty beef cross ribs
   (or substitute large lean
   short ribs)
garlic salt, or, better, use
   *Garlic Oil, Handy Dandy
   No. 1,* p. 3, and a little
   salt

1 package dried onion soup
1 (10¾-ounce) can
   condensed cream of
   onion soup
¼ cup sherry

Trim excess fat from the ribs. Season with garlic salt or with *Garlic Oil* and a little salt. Place in a roasting pan or Dutch oven.
Combine the remaining ingredients and pour over the meat.
Cover tightly and roast at 350° for 40 minutes. Reduce heat to
250° and roast about another 1½ hours, or until tender.

Ahead of time: I always do these a day ahead and chill overnight; then it is easy to remove congealed fat before reheating. And they freeze beautifully.

Mexican-Style Cross Ribs

[serves about 6]

4 to 5 pounds lean beef
   cross ribs (or substitute
   large lean short ribs)
salt
1 large onion, sliced

1 (8-ounce) can tomato
   sauce
1 (10-ounce) can enchilada
   sauce

Season the ribs with salt and place in a roasting pan or Dutch oven. Cover with the onion slices. Place, uncovered, in a 350° oven for 45 minutes. Pour the sauces over the meat, cover pan tightly, reduce heat to 250°, and cook for 2 to 3 hours, or until tender. Remove, cool, then chill overnight. Next day, remove congealed fat. Reheat and serve as desired.

Ahead of time: As directed in the recipe. These freeze well too.

Cross Ribs with Potatoes and Carrots

[serves 4]

4 large meaty beef cross ribs
   (or use large lean short
   ribs)
Garlic Oil, Handy Dandy
   No. 1, p. 3
salt and pepper
3 or 4 carrots, cut in 2-inch
   pieces

2 onions, quartered
2 large boiling potatoes,
   quartered
1 (10¾-ounce) can
   condensed cream of
   celery soup
½ cup dry red wine

Season the meat with *Garlic Oil*, salt, and pepper. Place in a large roasting pan and brown meat under a broiling unit for about 2 minutes on each side. Arrange the vegetables around the meat. Combine the soup and wine and pour over the meat and vegetables. Cover tightly with foil and bake at 275° for about 2½ to 3 hours. Remove and cool, then if possible chill overnight. The next day, remove congealed fat and arrange meat and vegetables in a large shallow casserole. Bake uncovered at 400° for about 30 to 45 minutes. Serve hot directly from casserole.

Ahead of time: These are really best done ahead of time, as directed in the recipe; in fact, they can be cooked several days ahead. They freeze well too.

No-Effort Brisket

[serves about 8]

3½ to 4 pounds lean brisket of beef
1 package dried mushroom soup

1 package dried onion soup
2½ cups dry white wine

Place the beef in a roasting pan. Combine the soups with the wine and pour over the meat. Cover pan tightly with a lid or foil. Roast (without looking and without basting) in a 225° or 250° oven for 10 to 12 hours. Remove from oven and remove fat that has accumulated. Slice the meat, return it to the sauce, reheat, and serve.

Ahead of time: This recipe obviously is perfect for overnight cooking; it cooks while you sleep. And it is even better if you start it two days ahead. Chill it during the second night and then it is easy to remove congealed fat.

Non-Rushed Brisket of Beef

[serves 8 to 10]

5½ to 6 pounds lean brisket of beef
1 large onion, sliced
1 (12-ounce) bottle chili sauce (Heinz)

3 tablespoons soy sauce
1½ cups dry white wine

Place the brisket in a large roasting pan. Cover with the remaining ingredients. Cover tightly with foil and roast at 300° for about 3 hours or until tender. Cool, then, if possible, chill overnight. Remove congealed fat, slice meat, then return the slices to the sauce. Reheat and serve.

Ahead of time: This can be prepared several days ahead; it also freezes well.

Brisket with Mustard and Onions

[serves 12 to 16]

1 large brisket of beef (about 8 pounds)
salt and pepper

¾ cup Dijon-style mustard
2 large onions, sliced
chopped parsley

Trim off as much fat as possible. Season the meat with salt and pepper and place in a large roasting pan which has a cover, or use heavy-duty foil to cover. Spread the top of the brisket with the mustard, then with the onions. Cover tightly and roast 3 to 4 hours, or until tender. Remove and cool, then chill overnight. Remove congealed fat, then slice meat and place in a very large casserole or in two smaller ones. Cover the slices with the sauce that created itself during the roasting. Reheat in a 325° oven for 30 minutes or longer—until very hot. Serve with a sprinkling of chopped fresh parsley and accompany with noodles or rice and a colorful fresh vegetable.

Ahead of time: This can be roasted 2 or 3 days ahead and kept refrigerated. It freezes beautifully, then can be divided into small quantities for family dinners. If possible defrost before reheating.

Tip: It is not necessary to baste this while it cooks.

Chuck Pot Roast with Potatoes

[serves about 6]

1 (3-pound) beef chuck
  roast
3 large boiling potatoes,
  peeled, then cut in half
  salt and pepper

1 onion, sliced
1 package dried onion soup
1 (10¾-ounce) can
  condensed cream of
  potato soup

Place the meat in a roasting pan and surround with the potatoes. Season with salt and pepper, then cover with the sliced onion and the combined soups. Cover tightly and place in a 350° oven. Roast for 20 minutes, then reduce oven to 225° and roast an additional 2 to 3 hours—until tender.

Ahead of time: Like most pot roasts, this benefits from day-ahead preparation. Chill overnight, then remove fat and remove and slice meat. Return meat to sauce and heat in a 325° oven. This can be frozen.

Chuck Pot Roast with Tomatoes

[serves about 6]

1 (3-pound) beef chuck
   roast
salt and pepper
1 (1-pound) can tomatoes

⅓ cup dry red wine
⅓ cup Minute tapioca
1 package dried onion soup

Combine all ingredients and place in a large ovenproof casserole. Cover and roast at 250° for 3½ to 4 hours.

Ahead of time: This is much better done one or two days ahead; remove fat and reheat meat before serving.

Aromatic and Easily Prepared Greek Stew

[serves about 6]

4 large onions, coarsely
   sliced
3 pounds stew beef, cut in
   2-inch pieces
½ cup melted butter
2 tablespoons flour
1 (6-ounce) can tomato
   paste

3 teaspoons salt (or to taste)
½ teaspoon pepper
1 teaspoon cinnamon
½ teaspoon cloves
½ teaspoon ground cumin
¾ cup dry red wine
¼ cup brown sugar
¼ cup raisins

Combine all ingredients in a large ovenproof casserole and stir. Cover and bake at 250° for 3 to 4 hours. Serve with white rice.

Ahead of time: This can be cooked the day before (or several days before) and reheated in a 300° oven. It freezes well too.

Unstuffed Cabbage

[serves about 6]

1½ pounds lean ground beef
1½ teaspoons salt
½ teaspoon pepper
3 tablespoons uncooked rice
¼ cup water
2 teaspoons dehydrated
   minced onion
2 eggs
1 medium-sized cabbage

1 (28-ounce) can tomatoes
1 (6-ounce) can tomato
   paste
½ cup brown sugar (pack to
   measure)
½ cup vinegar
2 tablespoons minced
   dehydrated onion

Combine the beef, salt, pepper, rice, water, 2 teaspoons dehydrated onion, and eggs; mix well. Shred the cabbage by slicing it coarsely. Make a sauce by combining the remaining ingredients. Place half the cabbage in a large shallow casserole (Pyrex or enamel or ceramic) and top with half the sauce. Make the meat mixture into about 12 balls and place them on the cabbage and sauce, then cover with remaining cabbage and sauce. (You may want to season the cabbage lightly with salt and pepper, but don't use too much.) Cover tightly with foil and bake at 325° for 1 hour, then reduce heat to 250° and bake 3 more hours. Remove from oven and cool, then refrigerate overnight. The next day, bring casserole to room temperature, then bake uncovered at 300° for 45 minutes. Serve hot with boiled potatoes or noodles.

Ahead of time: This clearly is a glorious ahead-of-time concoction. It can be eaten the same day but is ever so much better prepared as directed in the recipe. And it freezes divinely.

Tip: This closely approximates the taste of stuffed cabbage (Jewish sweet-and-sour style), but without the hours of preparation. I timed myself and found that with the ingredients on hand it took me less than 15 minutes to assemble the entire thing, and though the cooking takes many hours, it is looking after itself. Economical too.

Hamburger Chinese Style, Inspired by
Abe Mellinkoff's Recipe

[serves 3 or 4]

1 large onion, chopped
4 tablespoons butter
1 cup sliced celery
1 small green pepper,
   chopped
1 pound ground beef

salt and pepper
3 or more tablespoons soy
   sauce
2 teaspoons sesame seed oil
½ pound fresh bean sprouts

Sauté the onion in the butter, then add the celery and green pepper and sauté 1 or 2 minutes longer. Add the beef and break it up as it cooks; do all this over high heat. Add salt and pepper, the soy sauce, sesame seed oil, and bean sprouts. Toss and cook for about 2 or 3 more minutes. Serve very hot with cooked rice.

Ahead of time: Vegetables can be chopped and sliced in the morning, or the day before, and kept covered in the refrigerator. This reheats excellently the next day.

Tip: Abe likes to add a small (4½-ounce) can chopped ripe olives—juice and all—for added color and flavor.

Meat Balls and Sauerkraut, Sweet and Sour

[serves 10 to 12]

2 pounds lean beef chuck,
   ground twice
2 teaspoons salt
½ teaspoon pepper
½ cup dry bread crumbs
½ cup ketchup (Heinz)
2 teaspoons onion powder
1 egg
2 (1-pound) cans
   sauerkraut, undrained

2 onions, coarsely chopped
2 (1-pound) cans tomatoes,
   mashed or chopped,
   undrained
1¼ cups brown sugar (pack
   to measure)
½ cup lemon juice

Mix the ground chuck, salt, pepper, bread crumbs, ketchup, onion powder, and egg together thoroughly. Form into small meatballs. Using a large casserole, layer meat balls with sauerkraut and onion, ending with sauerkraut on top. Top with the chopped tomatoes and juice, the brown sugar, and the lemon juice. Cover tightly and bake at 275° for 3 hours. Uncover and bake ½ hour to 1 hour.

Ahead of time: Best if done the day before, then reheated for 1 hour or more in a 275° oven. This can be prepared 3 or 4 days ahead if kept well covered and refrigerated. It freezes well too.

Open-Face Spicy Hamburgers on Sour-Dough Bread

[serves about 4]

   soft butter
   sour-dough bread or large
      rolls, split in half
      lengthwise
1½ pounds ground beef
   chuck
1½ teaspoons salt

½ teaspoon pepper
1 onion, finely chopped
1 green pepper, finely
   chopped
1 cup chili sauce (Heinz)
1 tablespoon dry bread
   crumbs

Butter the split bread or rolls on the cut sides. Combine the remaining ingredients and mix well. Shortly before serving, cover the cut sides of bread or rolls about ½ inch thick, with the meat mixture. Broil about 5 minutes or so and serve at once.

Ahead of time: The meat mixture can be done the day before and kept refrigerated until an hour or so before you are ready to broil the hamburgers. Bring to room temperature if time permits, otherwise allow more time to cook the meat.

A Lazily Layered Ground-Beef Casserole

[serves 4 to 6]

1 large onion, sliced
1 cup sliced celery
1 green pepper, sliced
   salt and pepper
1¼ to 1½ pounds ground
   beef
1 (8-ounce) can tomato
   sauce

2 large potatoes, peeled and
   sliced
1 (10¾-ounce) can
   condensed cream of
   celery soup

Place layers of half the sliced onion, celery, and green pepper in a 2-quart casserole. Season with salt and pepper. Place ground beef on top of these and sprinkle with about ¾ teaspoon salt and ½ teaspoon pepper. Cover with tomato sauce. Place the remaining onion, celery, and green pepper on top of the tomato sauce and season with more salt and pepper. Arrange potato slices over this and cover with the soup. Bake uncovered in a 350° oven for 1½ to 2 hours. Do not stir. If desired you can press down on the top to release bottom juices—that is, to let them rise to the top.

Ahead of time: This can be done the day before and reheated. It can also be frozen; defrost, then reheat, covered, in a 350° oven.

Luciano's Lovely Veal Chops

[serves 6]

6 perfect veal chops, 1¼ to
   1½ inches thick
salt and pepper
olive oil

oregano
6 tablespoons sweet butter
lemon wedges

Season the chops with salt and pepper and rub with a generous amount of olive oil. Sprinkle with oregano. Let them stand at room temperature for 15 minutes to ½ hour (or longer). Broil or barbecue on the grill for about 7 minutes or so on each side. Veal should still be pinkish inside—neither rare nor well-done. Place on a very hot platter, top each chop with 1 tablespoon sweet butter, and serve each with one or two lemon wedges.

Tip: Really good veal is extremely difficult to find and very expensive. I have made this very successfully with beef sirloin and porterhouse steaks.

Butterflied Lamb Chops with Rosemary and Garlic

[serves 4]

4 thick French-cut lamb
   chops, butterflied (cut
   through almost to the
   bone, then opened and
   flattened)
salt and pepper

2 teaspoons rosemary
2 tablespoons butter
2 teaspoons mashed garlic
   and 3 tablespoons oil
   from *Garlic Oil, Handy
   Dandy No. 1,* p. 3.

Season the lamb chops with salt and pepper. Crush the rosemary and press it firmly into chops (about ½ teaspoon per chop). Heat the butter, garlic, and oil, then sauté chops quickly on both sides—they should remain pink inside. Serve at once.

Ahead of time: The important element to have ready ahead of time is the *Garlic Oil.*

A Splendidly Easy Way with Leftover Lamb

[serves about 6]

4 cups diced cooked lamb
2 cans condensed Scotch
   broth (Campbell's)
½ cup dry marsala or dry
   sherry

salt and pepper to taste
mashed potatoes (see
   *Iconoclastic Mashed
   Potatoes*, p. 181

Combine the lamb, soup, marsala, salt, and pepper. Place in a casserole and cover. Bake at 350° for 45 minutes. Remove cover and top with mashed potatoes. Increase oven heat to 425° and bake until lightly browned—about 15 minutes more.

Ahead of time: The lamb mixture can be cooked the day before or in the morning.

Tip: For further simplification you can eliminate the mashed potatoes; cook the lamb a little longer, then sprinkle with a little grated cheese and brown briefly.

French Hot Dogs

spicy frankfurters (kosher-
   style are probably the best
   in the U.S.A.)
long baguette-type French
   bread

sliced or grated imported
   swiss cheese or good
   cheddar
Dijon-style mustard

Cook the frankfurters in simmering water for 3 minutes. Cut the bread into pieces about 6 or 7 inches in length, then split them in half horizontally. Heat for about 3 minutes in a 350° oven. Remove from oven and fill with the frankfurters and some of the cheese. Return sandwiches to the oven just long enough to heat and crisp the bread (about 3 to 5 minutes). Serve at once, with the mustard on the side.

Eileen Taylor's Special Pork Chops

[serves 6]

6 lean pork chops, 1½
    inches thick
    salt
½ cup apple sauce

2 tablespoons ketchup
2 tablespoons soy sauce
    grated rind of 1 lemon

Place the chops in an ovenproof casserole and season lightly with salt. Combine remaining ingredients and cover the chops with this sauce. Bake, uncovered, at 350° for about 1 hour or a little longer. Pork must be cooked to the well-done stage.

Smoked Pork Chops, Baked

[serves 4]

4 large smoked pork chops,
    ½- to ¾-inch thick
½ cup Dijon-style mustard

¼ cup brown sugar
1 cup sour cream

Generously cover each chop, top and bottom, with mustard. Sprinkle each, top and bottom, with the sugar. Place in a casserole, side by side (do not layer them) and cover with the sour cream. Cover with foil and bake at 350° for about 50 to 60 minutes.

Ahead of time: These can be assembled in the morning to be baked in the evening.

Tip: Sautéed cabbage or buttered brussels sprouts make a fine accompaniment.

7/SPECIAL ENTRÉES

*pasta, rice, peas, and bean dishes;
casserole recipes; special sandwiches;
egg and cheese dishes; and other
miscellaneous concoctions*

Easy

A Cautiously Carefree Cassoulet

[serves 8 to 10]

2 onions, chopped
3 garlic cloves, mashed, plus about 3 tablespoons *Garlic Oil, Handy Dandy, No. 1*, p. 3
8 ounces small pork sausages
8 ounces cocktail-size kosher frankfurters, cut in halves (or larger ones cut in 1-inch pieces)
3 cups diced leftover roast lamb

¾ cup very rich lamb gravy (or canned beef bouillon)
3 (1-pound) cans baked beans (Heinz)
2 (1-pound) cans garbanzo beans, drained
2 (8-ounce) cans tomato sauce
1 tablespoon chopped parsley
salt and pepper to taste

Sauté the onions and garlic in the *Garlic Oil* until tender. Add the sausages and brown lightly. Add the remaining ingredients and mix thoroughly. Place in an ovenproof casserole and bake, uncovered, at 300° for 1 hour or more. Serve very hot.

Ahead of time: This can be done the day before. Keep refrigerated but if possible bring to room temperature before reheating. This can be frozen. Defrost and heat as directed above.

Superlative Corn and Green Chile Casserole

[serves 8]

2 (10-ounce) packages
   frozen kernel corn
½ cup melted butter
2 eggs, beaten
½ cup yellow cornmeal
1¼ teaspoons salt
1 cup sour cream

1 generous cup diced jack
   cheese (about 7 or 8
   ounces)
1 (4-ounce) can green
   chiles, seeded and
   chopped

Defrost the corn. Grind it in a blender or a food processor, then place in a large bowl. Add the remaining ingredients. Pour into a greased casserole and bake at 350° for 40 to 60 minutes, or until firm to the touch and golden brown.

Ahead of time: This can be baked the day before or in the morning, then reheated before serving. It is also delicious served cold for lunch with a green salad. This freezes superbly; to serve, defrost, then reheat in oven.

Tip: Very special since it serves both as a starch and a vegetable. Serve with baked ham or broiled chicken, or with roast beef or lamb.

A Wild Casserole of Wild Rice and Shrimp for Many Wild Ones

[serves 40 to 50 at a buffet with other dishes]

1 cup chopped green
   onions
2 chopped green peppers
3 cups chopped celery
3 cups sour cream
   juice of 2 lemons
4 teaspoons salt (or more)
1 teaspoon pepper
4 teaspoons curry powder

6 cups mayonnaise, or a
   little more
½ teaspoon oregano
½ teaspoon thyme
4 quarts (16 cups) cooked
   wild rice
7 to 8 pounds cooked and
   peeled shrimp

Combine all ingredients, taste for seasoning, cover with foil, and heat in a 350° oven for about 1 hour—only until very hot.

Ahead of time: This can be mixed the day before and refrigerated, well covered. Bring to room temperature and heat as directed.

Tip: Wildly expensive, but can be reduced in quantity for smaller gatherings, and reduced in expense by using only part wild rice and part brown or white rice.

Deviled Eggs with Shrimp Sauce

[serves 3 or 4]

6 hard-boiled eggs
4 tablespoons mayonnaise

1 or 2 teaspoons mustard
salt and pepper

for sauce

2 tablespoons butter
2 tablespoons flour
½ teaspoon salt
⅛ teaspoon pepper
1 cup milk

¼ cup sherry
¾ cup grated cheddar
   cheese
1 cup tiny cooked shrimp
   (about 4 ounces)

Remove egg yolks and mash, then combine to taste with mayonnaise, mustard, salt, and pepper. Stuff the eggs and place in small individual baking dishes or in one large dish. To make the sauce, melt the butter, stir in the flour, salt and pepper, and gradually add the milk, stirring until it comes to a boil. Add the sherry, then over very low heat stir in the cheese. Remove from heat, add the shrimp and cool slightly. Spoon over stuffed eggs. Bake at 350° until hot and browned—about 15 to 20 minutes. If desired, a browner top can be achieved by placing under a broiling unit for 1 or 2 minutes.

Ahead of time: These can be completely assembled the day before or in the morning. Keep refrigerated, but bring to room temperature before baking.

Italian Foundation for Frivolities and Follies

3 or 4 cloves garlic,
mashed, or garlic from
*Garlic Oil, Handy Dandy
No. 1,* p. 3
4 onions, chopped
½ cup olive oil
2 cups canned stewed
tomatoes
4 cups canned tomato purée
1 (6-ounce) can tomato
paste

½ cup dry red wine
1½ cups beef stock (canned
bouillon okay)
1½ teaspoons salt (about)
½ teaspoon pepper
1 tablespoon sugar
1 teaspoon basil
½ teaspoon oregano
½ teaspoon thyme

Sauté the garlic and onions in the olive oil for 5 to 10 minutes. Add the remaining ingredients and simmer for 1½ to 2 hours. Taste for seasoning.

Ahead of time: This can be made days ahead or in the morning; just reheat before using. The sauce freezes very well. It can of course be made in larger quantities.

Tip: Cook your favorite pasta, then serve this sauce with any of the following: meatballs; sautéed chicken livers; diced baked ham; sautéed jumbo shrimp; lots of grated parmesan cheese; lobster combined with crabmeat; sautéed pork chops; canned tuna broken into large pieces.

Triple Alfredo

*[makes about 3 quarts sauce—enough for 3 pounds pasta,
or about 12 generous servings]*

3 onions, chopped
6 tablespoons *Garlic Oil,
  Handy Dandy, No. 1*, p.
  3
3 pounds lean ground beef
  (or part lean ground
  pork)
1 pound fresh mushrooms,
  sliced (or use canned)
⅓ cup flour
6 cups beef stock (canned
  or made from bouillon
  cubes)

1 (6-ounce) can tomato
  paste
1 (8-ounce) can tomato
  sauce
2 cups canned tomato purée
  salt and pepper to taste
1 teaspoon oregano
2 tablespoons soy sauce
3 tablespoons chopped
  parsley
6 tablespoons grated
  parmesan cheese

Sauté the onions in the *Garlic Oil* until tender. Add the beef and
cook, stirring, until browned. Add the mushrooms and cook 1
minute. Sprinkle with the flour and stir. Add the remaining ingredients and bring to a boil, stirring occasionally. Cook over
low heat, covered, for 1½ hours. Uncover and cook about 1
more hour. Stir occasionally to prevent bottom from scorching.
Taste for seasoning.

Ahead of time: This can be made several days ahead and kept
refrigerated. And by all means freeze some.

Chiles Rellenos Scrumptious and Easy

[serves 10 to 12]

15 to 16 ounces canned green chiles

1 pound cheddar cheese, sliced (Herkimer County if you can find it)

1 pound jack cheese, sliced

4 tablespoons (¼ cup) flour

½ teaspoon salt

1 (13-ounce) can evaporated milk (Carnation)

4 extra-large eggs

2 (8-ounce) cans tomato sauce

Open the chiles and remove seeds. Place half of them in the bottom of a large shallow casserole (I use a round one about 12 inches in diameter and 2½ inches deep; or try a Pyrex casserole about 9 by 12 inches). Cover with all the sliced cheddar. Top with the remaining chiles, then cover with all the sliced jack cheese. Beat the flour and salt with a small amount of the evaporated milk to make a paste, then beat in the remaining milk. Add the eggs and beat again. Pour over chiles and cheese and bake in a 325° oven for about 1 hour. Pour the tomato sauce over the top and continue baking about 20 to 30 minutes.

Ahead of time: This lends itself magnificently to ahead-of-time preparation. It can be assembled the day before without the milk-egg mixture and refrigerated, to be baked the next day. Or it can be baked completely the day before, since it reheats extremely well. Or it can be baked in the morning and reheated in the evening. And it freezes too. Freeze after baking, then defrost completely and reheat.

Two Chicken Tortilla Casseroles

*[serves 18 to 20; you can, of course,
divide the recipe to make only one]*

16 chicken breasts
½ cup water
   salt
2 onions, chopped
¼ cup butter
2 (10¾-ounce) cans
   condensed cream of
   mushroom soup
2 (10¾-ounce) cans
   condensed cream of
   chicken soup
2 (4-ounce) cans green
   chiles, seeded and
   chopped, or 1 (7-ounce)
   can chile salsa

3 cups stock (from cooking
   chicken, plus milk if
   necessary)
2 dozen tortillas, cut in
   sixths
2 pounds grated cheese
   (cheddar, jack, or swiss,
   or a combination)

Cook the chicken breasts in a covered casserole or baking pan with ½ cup water and a little salt in a 325° oven for about 1 hour. Chill, then skin, bone, and break chicken into large pieces. Reserve the stock. Sauté the onions gently in the butter, then add the canned soups, chiles, and the stock. Spread two casseroles (large, shallow Pyrex ones are nice for this) with a layer of sauce, then layers of chicken, tortillas, and cheese; repeat layers, ending with cheese on top. Cover with foil and bake at 300°, then remove foil to brown lightly.

Ahead of time: This can be assembled in the morning or the day before, then baked before serving. Or it can be baked the day before and refrigerated. It reheats beautifully, and freezes well too.

Tip: Perfect for party buffets, but also lovely for family dinners; quantities can be cut in half or even in quarters.

Easier

Fettucine Facile

[serves 4 as a main course; 6 to 8 as a first course]

½ pound butter
2 cups heavy cream
1 teaspoon salt
½ teaspoon pepper

½ pound grated parmesan
   cheese (about 2 cups)
12 ounces fettucine

for pasta

8 quarts water
2 tablespoons oil

2 tablespoons salt

Melt the butter in a saucepan (but don't let it cook). Add the cream over low heat and barely warm it, then remove from heat and stir in the salt, pepper, and grated parmesan. Set aside. For the pasta, bring the water to a boil in a large pot, then add oil and salt. Add fettucine and cook until just barely tender (*al dente*). Drain but do not rinse. Return fettucine to the pot and pour the butter-cream mixture over it. Toss thoroughly over lowest possible heat for about 1 or 2 minutes. Serve on heated plates. You can pass additional grated parmesan but it really doesn't need it.

Ahead of time: The butter-cream-parmesan mixture can be readied in the morning and left covered at room temperature.

Tip: The proportions have been exactly worked out; if you change them, the taste will not be the same.

Tuna, Olives, and Shrimp with Spaghetti

[serves 2 or 3 as a main course;
4 to 6 as a first course]

½ cup small green pitted
    olives ("salad" olives)
1 (7-ounce) can tuna fish,
    drained
1 cup diced cooked shrimp
2 cups *Tomato Sauce, Style*
    A, Handy Dandy No. 11,
    p. 10

4 quarts boiling water
1 teaspoon salt
1 tablespoon oil
½ pound thin spaghetti

Add the olives, tuna, and shrimp to *Tomato Sauce* and heat gently. To 4 quarts of boiling water add 1 tablespoon salt and 1 tablespoon oil and add the spaghetti. Cook to the *al dente* stage. Drain, but do not rinse. Place on a large hot platter or in a hot casserole. Serve each guest some of the spaghetti, then top with some of the sauce.

Ahead of time: The *Tomato Sauce* can easily be made ahead of time.

Tip: This can be made with double the quantity of tuna omitting the shrimp.

Clams with Spaghetti

[serves 2 or 3 as a main course;
about 4 to 6 as a first course]

1 garlic clove, mashed, or
    garlic from *Garlic Oil,*
    Handy Dandy, No. 1, p.
    3
½ cup olive oil
½ teaspoon salt
½ teaspoon freshly ground
    pepper
½ teaspoon oregano

1 (10-ounce) can whole
    baby clams
1 (8-ounce) can minced
    clams
½ pound thin spaghetti
¼ cup butter
    chopped parsley
    more freshly ground
    pepper at table

Sauté garlic in olive oil for about 2 minutes. Add salt, pepper, oregano, and juice from all clams. Simmer 2 minutes and set aside. Cook the spaghetti *al dente*. Drain but do not rinse. Put back in pot, add butter, and toss. Heat all clams gently in the sauce, then add all to spaghetti, add chopped parsley, and toss for about 2 to 3 minutes over lowest heat. Serve at table and pass freshly ground pepper or the pepper mill.

Ahead of time: The clam sauce can be prepared the day before or in the morning and kept refrigerated. Reheat gently while cooking the spaghetti.

Italian Green Noodles with Ricotta, Raisins, and Rum

[serves about 10]

1 cup seedless raisins, washed and dried	1 pound ricotta cheese
½ cup light rum	2 cups heavy cream
1 pound Italian green noodles, cooked *al dente*	2 to 3 teaspoons salt
	1 teaspoon pepper

Soak the raisins in the rum. Combine all ingredients and place in a large casserole. Cover lightly with foil. Bake at 350° for 20 to 25 minutes, just long enough to heat—don't overcook.

Ahead of time: Raisins, rum, ricotta, cream, salt, and pepper can be combined in the morning and left at room temperature. Noodles can be cooked several hours ahead; drain but do not rinse. Combine all and place in casserole just before heating. While this can be reheated the next day, it is not at its best. The same applies to freezing; however, save leftovers either in the refrigerator or freezer for family use.

Spinach-Noodle Bake

[serves about 6]

4 ounces wide noodles,
   cooked only until barely
   tender
1 (10-ounce) package frozen
   chopped spinach,
   defrosted and well
   drained
½ onion, chopped

3 tablespoons butter
2 eggs
1 cup sour cream
¾ teaspoon salt
¼ teaspoon pepper
¼ cup grated parmesan
   cheese

Combine the noodles and spinach in a bowl. Sauté the onion in the butter in a skillet until tender, then add to noodles. Beat the eggs with the sour cream, salt, and pepper. Add to the noodle mixture along with the grated parmesan. Mix well. Spoon into a buttered 8-inch-square pan. Bake at 350° for 30 to 40 minutes.

Ahead of time: This can be completely mixed in the morning and left at room temperature, covered with plastic wrap. Mix again gently before baking. Pour into square pan and bake as directed in recipe.

Chicken Livers Marsala

[serves 4 as a main course; more as an hors d'oeuvre]

1 pound fresh chicken livers
   flour
¼ cup butter

salt and pepper
½ cup marsala (dry or
   sweet)

Cut the livers in half and roll in flour. Sauté in butter just until tender, about 5 to 7 minutes. Season with salt and pepper. Add the marsala, cover pan, and simmer over lowest heat for about 2 to 3 minutes. Serve hot.

Ahead of time: These can be prepared in the morning. Do not refrigerate; just cover and leave at room temperature. Reheat in a skillet over lowest heat.

Tip: These make a marvelous hot hors d'oeuvre; transfer livers to a chafing dish to keep warm and let guests help themselves.

Gertie Lee Short's Barbecued Beans

[serves 18 to 25]

2 onions, chopped
½ cup butter
2 (8-ounce) cans tomato
    sauce
1 cup tomato ketchup
½ cup Worcestershire sauce
½ cup prepared mustard
¼ cup prepared horseradish

6 tablespoons brown sugar
2 teaspoons salt
1 teaspoon paprika
3 tablespoons vinegar
5 large cans (about 1-
    pound, 4-ounce size)
    kidney beans, drained

Sauté the onions in the butter in a skillet until golden. Add all remaining ingredients except the beans and simmer about 30 minutes. Mix sauce with beans and bake in a large casserole for about 1½ to 2 hours at 325°.

Ahead of time: This can be prepared completely several days before or in the morning. These beans can be frozen; reheat after defrosting.

Tip: These are splendid and unusual for a large buffet; excellent with baked ham or smoked tongue.

A Versatile Cheese Entrée for Lunch, Supper, or Appetizer

[serves 8 as an entrée, 16 or more as an appetizer]

10 slices white bread
    softened butter
¾ pound cheddar cheese,
    grated
¾ pound jack cheese or
    fontina, grated
8 eggs, slightly beaten
3 to 4 cups light cream
1 teaspoon brown sugar

¼ teaspoon paprika
1½ teaspoons salt
½ teaspoon onion powder
¼ teaspoon pepper
⅛ teaspoon cayenne
1 teaspoon Worcestershire
    sauce
1 teaspoon dry mustard

Butter the bread, then cut in cubes. Line a large shallow baking dish with half the bread cubes. Sprinkle with half the cheese, then repeat: bread and cheese. Combine the remaining ingredients and pour over the bread and cheese. Refrigerate 8 to 24 hours. Bake in a 325° oven for about 1 hour or more. Serve hot as an entrée (or cold if you like it so); or cut in small squares and serve as an appetizer.

Ahead of time: This is best if assembled the day before and baked the next day. It can also be reheated after baking. This can be frozen; freeze after baking, defrost, then reheat.

Tip: It is easier to cut this into small squares for appetizers if it is baked, chilled, and then cut. To serve as a hot appetizer, place the small squares on baking sheets, heat in a 350° oven, then serve with toothpicks.

Mary Cullins' Black-eyed Peas

[serves about 8]

¾ pound smoked bacon, in
   one piece
1 pound dried black-eyed
   peas
5 cups boiling water

2 garlic cloves, whole
1 teaspoon salt (may need
   more)
1 tablespoon sugar
¾ pound chorizo sausage

Cut the bacon into largish cubes and place in a Dutch oven. Pick over the peas and discard bad ones along with any foreign objects, such as pebbles. Add peas to bacon and pour the boiling water over them. Add the garlic, salt, and sugar. Cover and place in a 350° oven for about 1½ hours. Add the chorizos, cut in chunks, re-cover and return to oven for about 45 minutes. Taste for seasoning and add more salt if needed. Remove the cover and return to oven for about another 45 minutes. Remove from oven and skim off excess fat. Serve hot with cornbread.

Ahead of time: This can be prepared several days ahead and kept refrigerated; and it freezes divinely.

Tip: This delicious treat ought not to be overlooked since it is easy to make and stores so well either in the refrigerator or freezer.

Moon-Madness Turkey Enchiladas

[makes 6, 12, or 24 servings]

	Six	Twelve	Twenty-four
diced turkey	1½ cups	3 cups	6 cups
sour cream	¼ cup	½ cup	1 cup
mayonnaise	¼ cup	½ cup	1 cup
garlic salt	½ teaspoon	1 teaspoon	2 teaspoons
cheese, half cheddar and half jack or swiss	½ pound	1 pound	2 pounds
salt and pepper (to taste)			
corn tortillas	6	12	24
for the sauce			
butter	¼ cup	½ cup	1 cup
flour	¼ cup	½ cup	1 cup
enchilada sauce (10-ounce can)	1 can	2 cans	4 cans
chicken stock	2½ cups	5 cups	10 cups
dehydrated minced onion	1 tablespoon	2 tablespoons	4 tablespoons

To make the sauce, melt the butter, stir in the flour, gradually add enchilada sauce and stock, then stir until sauce boils. Add the onion and simmer gently for 5 minutes.

Combine the diced turkey with the sour cream, mayonnaise, garlic salt, half the cheese, and salt and pepper. Divide among the tortillas. Roll them up and place seam-side-down in casseroles or foil pans. Cover with sauce and top with the remaining cheese. Bake uncovered at 350° until hot (about 15 to 20 minutes when everything is at room temperature; longer if they have been refrigerated or frozen).

Ahead of time: These can be done the day before or in the morning and refrigerated; they can also be frozen. Defrost, then reheat.

Tip: After these are heated, they can be garnished with sour cream and chopped green onions.

Cheese and Chiles

[serves about 4 for lunch, more as an appetizer]

4 large eggs	1 teaspoon salt (scant)
1 (4-ounce) can green chiles, seeded and chopped	1 cup (½ pint) cottage cheese
¼ cup flour	½ pound jack cheese, grated
1 teaspoon baking powder	¼ cup melted butter

Beat the eggs, then add the other ingredients and mix until well combined. Spoon into a lightly greased baking pan (9 by 9 inches). Bake at 400° for 10 minutes, then reduce temperature to 350° and bake an additional 40 minutes. Cut in large squares and serve hot.

Ahead of time: Ingredients can be readied—chiles seeded and chopped, jack cheese grated. This reheats well and is really quite good cold the next day.

Tip: Cut this in bite-sized pieces to serve as a hot appetizer.

Easiest

Jet-Age Casserole

[serves about 8]

4 cups sauerkraut, rinsed
   and thoroughly drained
4 (8-ounce) packages kosher
   cocktail frankfurters

4 cups sour cream
chopped parsley

Place the sauerkraut, frankfurters, and sour cream in layers in a deep casserole. Cover and bake at 350° for 2 hours; reduce heat to 275° and bake 1 more hour. Stir once during the baking period and again just before serving. Garnish with chopped parsley.

Ahead of time: This can be done in the morning or the day before. If it has been refrigerated, bring to room temperature before reheating.

Tip: This is a marvelous addition to a buffet. If you cannot find the kosher cocktail frankfurters, cut any fine-quality frankfurters in 2-inch pieces.

My Best Welsh Rarebit

¼ cup butter
¼ cup flour
½ teaspoon salt (or to taste)
3 teaspoons dry mustard
1¼ cups milk
1¼ cups beer

½ cup dry sherry
3 or 4 teaspoons
   Worcestershire sauce
2 pounds well-aged cheddar
   cheese, grated

Melt the butter, stir in the flour, salt, and dry mustard, then gradually add the milk, stirring constantly until mixture boils. Add the beer, sherry, and Worcestershire sauce and simmer for several minutes. Over lowest heat stir in the grated cheese and keep stirring until it is melted. Set aside or refrigerate until ready to use.

Ahead of time: This should keep in the refrigerator for several weeks; use as needed by gently rewarming it, stirring constantly. And it freezes very well.

Tip: Quantities can be cut in half, but this is a superb item to have on hand. Excellent served on toasted English muffins, topped with crisp bacon and surrounded by sliced tomatoes.

Fresh Tomato, Frankfurter, and Bean Casserole

[serves 3 to 6]

1 (1-pound) can baked
   beans (Heinz)
⅓ cup ketchup (Heinz)
1 teaspoon prepared
   mustard

1 onion, sliced
1 large tomato, sliced
6 kosher frankfurters

Mix the beans with ketchup and mustard and place in a casserole. Cover with sliced onion and tomato and top with the frankfurters. Bake at 350° for about 45 minutes.

Ahead of time: Can be assembled the day before or in the morning, then baked just before serving.

Gingered Rice

[serves 4 to 6]

1 cup raw rice
1¼ cups water

½ teaspoon salt
1 tablespoon butter

for later

2 tablespoons butter
¼ cup chopped candied
   ginger

¼ cup finely chopped green
   onion

Combine the rice, water, salt, and 1 tablespoon butter in a very heavy pan with a tight-fitting cover. Cover, bring to a boil, then simmer on lowest heat, still covered, for 15 to 18 minutes. Do not overcook. This should be *al dente*—that is, slightly under-done. Remove from heat and stir in the 2 tablespoons butter, the chopped ginger, and the green onions.

Ahead of time: This can be prepared the day before or in the morning. (Refrigerate if you like, but bring to room temperature before heating.) To reheat, place in a casserole, cover with foil, and bake in a 325° oven until very hot—about 20 minutes.

Tip: If you do not have a really heavy saucepan with a really tight-fitting cover, you may have to cook the rice with 1½ cups or 1⅔ cups water. You will just have to experiment.

Rice, Green-Chile, Jack-Cheese, and Sour-Cream Heaven

[serves 6]

3 cups cooked rice
2 cups sour cream
1 teaspoon salt
1 (4-ounce) can green
  chiles, seeded and
  chopped

½ pound jack cheese (or
  fontina, swiss, or
  cheddar), sliced or
  grated

Place 1 cup of the rice in the bottom of a 1½-quart casserole. Mix the sour cream with the salt and chiles and put one-third of the mixture on top of the rice. Add a layer of cheese. Repeat this procedure twice. Cover and bake at 350° for about 20 minutes. Uncover and bake another 10 minutes.

Ahead of time: This can be assembled the day before or in the morning, then baked before serving. It can be frozen; freeze it unbaked, defrost, then proceed with the baking.

Be-Prepared Fiesta Rolls

[makes 6]

6 large French sour-dough
   rolls
6 or 7 ounces cheddar
   cheese, grated
2 (2¼-ounce) cans ripe
   olives, pitted and sliced
   (1 cup)
1 small bunch green onions,
   chopped

½ green pepper, chopped
1 (8-ounce) can tomato
   sauce
2 tablespoons wine vinegar
½ cup olive oil
   salt (about ½ teaspoon)
   pepper (about ¼
   teaspoon)

Cut a lid from the top of each roll. Scoop out some of the soft insides. Combine the other ingredients and fill the rolls. Replace the tops. Wrap each roll in waxed paper (not foil) and refrigerate. When ready to use, place the rolls in their paper wrapping on a baking pan and heat in a 300° oven for about 30 minutes, or until very hot.

Ahead of time: These can be made 1 or 2 days ahead and kept refrigerated.

Tip: This recipe can easily be doubled—nice to have in the refrigerator for a long week-end of lunches.

Variation on a Reuben Theme

[makes 4 giant sandwiches]

4 kosher knockwurst, or your favorite large frankfurters	sliced cheese (cheddar or swiss)
soft butter	½ cup *Russian Dressing, Handy Dandy, No. 8*, p. 8
8 extra-large medium-thick slices New York style rye bread	1 cup well-drained sauerkraut

Cook the knockwurst or frankfurters, drain, and slice them about ⅛- to ¼-inch thick. Butter the bread generously on both sides. Place four buttered slices on a large baking sheet. Cover with cheese slices and add a spoonful of *Russian Dressing* on each. Add a small amount of sauerkraut, then a layer of sliced knockwurst or frankfurters, then a bit more *Russian Dressing* and another layer of cheese slices. Cover each with one of the remaining buttered bread slices. Heat oven to 400°. Place baking sheet on the rack at the lowest level and bake about 10 minutes. Move to topmost level and bake about another 10 to 15 minutes—until somewhat toasted. Serve hot with forks and knives.

Ahead of time: These can be assembled in the morning. Cover with plastic wrap until time to bake. (They even reheat remarkably well.)

Tip: Marvelous and filling for a Sunday supper gathering of hungry friends, good with very cold beer. Even easier, use sliced kosher salami instead of knockwurst or frankfurters.

Monte Cristo Sandwiches Ever So Simple

[serves 4]

12 slices white bread	thin slices of jack cheese
softened butter	(or cheddar or swiss)
sliced meat of chicken or	3 eggs
turkey	⅓ cup milk
salt and pepper	butter for cooking
thin slices of ham (boiled	strawberry jam
or baked)	

Remove crusts from bread. Butter 4 slices of bread on one side, then cover them with chicken or turkey and season lightly. Butter four more slices on both sides, place on top of the chicken or turkey, then put a layer of ham and one of cheese on top of the middle slices. Butter four more slices on one side and place buttered side down over the cheese. Cut sandwiches in half and fasten each half with a toothpick. Beat the eggs with the milk. Dip the sandwiches in the egg mixture and place them on a plate. Sauté both sides in butter in a skillet until browned. Serve hot with strawberry jam on the side.

Ahead of time: The sandwiches can be assembled the day before or in the morning, wrapped well, and kept in the refrigerator. Dip and sauté just before serving.

Tip: These can also be made with just chicken or turkey and cheese, or with just ham and cheese.

Pita Pizza

[makes 6 pizzas about 7 or 8 inches in diameter]

¼ cup melted butter
¼ cup *Garlic Oil, Handy Dandy No. 1, p. 3.*
3 large pita breads, split
1 (6-ounce) can tomato paste
salt and pepper

6 slices cheese (mozzarella or fontina or jack or swiss)
1 small can flat anchovies
2 slices salami or pepperoni sliced ripe olives
oregano

Combine the butter and *Garlic Oil.* Spread on the inside (rough side) of each split pita bread. Coat with tomato paste, then season with salt and pepper. Cover with sliced cheese. On two of the pita halves scatter anchovies; on another two, spread salami or pepperoni; and on the remaining two scatter sliced olives. Sprinkle all with some oregano. Bake in a 400° oven for 10 to 20 minutes (depending on whether or not they were refrigerated). Serve hot with forks and knives, or cut in quarters and serve as finger food.

Ahead of time: These can be assembled the day before, covered, and refrigerated, or they can be assembled in the morning and left at room temperature, covered. They reheat beautifully the next day.

Tip: Cut into small portions, these make lovely appetizers.

8/VEGETABLES

Easy

Jo Anne Cotsen's Very Special Artichokes

[*serves 4*]

4 large artichokes
4 garlic cloves, peeled, or
   mashed garlic from
   Garlic Oil, Handy Dandy
   No. 1, p. 3
salt

¾ cup olive oil
1 tablespoon oregano
1 tablespoon thyme
¼ cup chopped parsley
   melted butter flavored
   with garlic

Thoroughly soak the artichokes in water. Cut the tops off about one-fourth to one-third of the way from the top. Trim the bottoms. Deep in the center of each put 1 large garlic clove or some mashed garlic. Place the artichokes in a large pot, cover the bottom with about 1 inch of water, and add a little salt. Dribble olive oil over the tops. Divide the oregano and thyme over the artichokes, then cover pot tightly and bring to a boil. Reduce heat and simmer for about 1 hour or until almost tender. Sprinkle with parsley and continue cooking until tender. Serve hot with garlic-flavored butter.

Ahead of time: These can be precooked, but undercook somewhat. Cook on higher heat until tender (about ½ hour) before serving.

Do-Ahead Broccoli

[*serves about 6*]

1½ pounds fresh broccoli
   (about 4 cups cooked)
2 tablespoons butter
2 tablespoons flour
2 cups chicken stock
   salt and pepper

⅓ cup dry bread crumbs
½ cup grated parmesan
   cheese
⅓ cup sliced toasted
   almonds

Cook the broccoli to the crisp-tender stage and drain immediately. Place in a large shallow casserole and set aside. Melt the butter, stir in the flour, then add the stock, stirring constantly, until the sauce boils. Reduce the heat and simmer for 2 minutes, adding salt and pepper to taste. Set aside. Combine the crumbs and cheese and set aside. Before serving, cover the broccoli with the sauce and sprinkle with the crumbs and cheese. Top with the almonds. Bake uncovered at about 375° for 20 to 45 minutes (depending on temperature of broccoli and sauce)—but only until hot and lightly browned.

Ahead of time: The broccoli and sauce can be prepared the day before and refrigerated. Bring to room temperature an hour or so before baking, then add crumbs-cheese mixture and almonds and proceed as directed.

Eggplants with Colorful Peppers

[serves 6 to 12]

6 small eggplants (the long narrow type called Japanese eggplants in the United States)
olive oil
1 large onion, sliced

1 each: green pepper, red sweet pepper, and yellow sweet pepper, sliced (or use 3 green peppers)
salt and pepper

Wash the eggplants and trim, but do not peel. Cut them in half lengthwise, rub generously with olive oil, and season with salt. Place them cut side down in a baking pan and add a bit more oil to the pan. Bake at 450° for 30 minutes. Meanwhile, sauté the onion and the peppers in a small amount of olive oil and season with salt and pepper. Don't overcook. Remove eggplants from oven and place in a shallow casserole, cut sides up. Top each with some of the onion-peppers mixture. Just before serving place in a 375° oven for about 20 minutes, or until very hot.

Ahead of time: This can be prepared in the morning or the day before, but reserve the final baking until just before serving.

Green Peas with Red and Green Peppers

[serves about 4]

1½ cups shelled fresh peas 　　salt and pepper 2 tablespoons butter 2 tablespoons olive oil 1 green sweet pepper, 　　coarsely chopped	1 red sweet pepper, 　　coarsely chopped 3 green onions, chopped

Cook the peas about 2 or 3 minutes in boiling water. Drain, then season with salt, pepper, and butter. Set aside. Shortly before serving, heat the olive oil in a skillet. Add the peppers and onions and sauté over high heat for about 1 or 2 minutes (toss and stir while cooking). Add the peas and toss and stir for about another minute, or until peas are hot. Taste for seasoning.

Ahead of time: The peas can be cooked, and the other vegetables chopped, in the morning. Finish the cooking shortly before serving.

Tip: I prefer fresh peas, but frozen ones can be used for this.

Easy Potatoes Anna

[serves 6 to 8]

7 cups sliced baking 　　potatoes	salt and pepper ½ cup melted butter

Arrange the sliced potatoes in a shallow casserole in layers with salt, pepper, and butter. Bake, uncovered, in a 425° oven for 1 hour or 1½ hours. Potatoes should be well browned both on top and bottom.

Ahead of time: These can be baked in the morning. Remove from oven and cool at room temperature. Cover and leave at room temperature. Before serving, return to oven (uncovered) until very hot. (Or slice the potatoes in the morning and keep them immersed in ice water until time to bake. Drain and dry thoroughly on paper towels and proceed as directed.)

Baked French Fries

1 baking potato per person
salad oil (about 1 or 2
    tablespoons per potato)
  salt

Peel the potatoes, then cut as for French fries, and place in cold water. Drain, dry well on paper towels. Place in a bowl, pour salad oil over, and toss, using your hands. Scatter the potatoes in a shallow baking pan large enough to hold them in a single layer and place in a 450° oven for 45 minutes to 1 hour. Stir and turn potatoes once during their baking. When done, remove from oven, salt them, and serve very hot on a heated platter or dish.

Ahead of time: Potatoes can be peeled and cut in the morning but must be kept immersed in ice water until time to cook.

Tip: Make lots; there are never enough of these.

Whipped Potatoes Mysterious

[serves about 8]

2 packages instant mashed
  potatoes (French's),
  prepared with ¼ cup
  less water per package
  than instructions call for
½ cup melted butter
3 ounces cream cheese,
  diced

1 small can pimentos,
  drained and chopped
1 green pepper, chopped
3 green onions, chopped
½ cup grated parmesan
  cheese
1 cup grated cheddar
  cheese

Mix the prepared mashed potatoes with the other ingredients. Place in an ovenproof casserole. Bake uncovered at 350° for about 30 minutes or so.

Ahead of time: This can be assembled in the morning, covered, and refrigerated. Bring to room temperature about 1 to 2 hours before baking.

Yams Mashed and Baked with Pecans and Raisins

[serves 12 to 16, but recipe can easily be reduced]

8 cups mashed yams
¾ teaspoon salt (or to your taste)
½ cup melted butter
1 cup brown sugar (pack to measure)
2 teaspoons cinnamon

2 teaspoons nutmeg
1½ cups raisins, washed in warm water, then drained well
6 eggs, beaten
2 to 3 cups toasted pecans

Combine all ingredients and spoon into either one very large casserole or two medium-sized ones. Bake, uncovered, at 350° for about 45 minutes to 1 hour.

Ahead of time: This can be prepared in the morning or the day before, or it can be frozen. Plan to bring to room temperature if possible, then bake until very hot.

Tip: This quantity is planned for huge holiday turkeys and large gatherings of the clan; it is also splendid for any buffet party, served, for example, with a baked ham. But it is equally delicious made in a much smaller quantity and served with something like broiled chicken halves or baked game hens.

Easier

Celery Root and Potato Purée Simplified

[serves 4 to 6]

1 celery root (medium to
large size), peeled and
cut in ½-inch slices
1 package instant mashed
potatoes (French's)

4 tablespoons butter
salt and pepper to taste

Cook the celery root until tender (about 20 minutes). Drain and put through a food mill. Prepare the potatoes as directed on the package. Combine with the celery root, then add butter and seasonings. Serve hot.

Ahead of time: This can be prepared in the morning. Reheat either in a double boiler or in a 325° oven in a casserole tightly covered with foil.

Eggplant Simplicity with Onion, Green Pepper, and Tomato

[serves about 6]

1 medium-sized eggplant,
peeled, then cut in ½-
inch slices
salt and pepper

1 onion, sliced
1 green pepper, sliced
2 tomatoes, sliced

for the sauce
½ cup oil
½ cup ketchup (Heinz)

¼ cup vinegar

Place the eggplant slices in a large shallow casserole. Season with salt and pepper. Cover with the onion and green pepper slices. Season again. Top with the tomato slices. Combine the sauce ingredients and pour over all. Cover tightly with foil and bake at 325° for 1 hour, then uncover and bake for another 45 minutes. Serve hot or chilled; this is delicious either hot as a vegetable or cold as a salad or hors d'oeuvre.

Ahead of time: This can be prepared the day before and either served chilled or reheated.

Iconoclastic Mashed Potatoes

[serves 4 to 6]

1¼ cups water
½ cup milk
½ teaspoon salt
1 package instant mashed
    potatoes (French's)

2 tablespoons mayonnaise
1 egg
1 tablespoon Dijon-style
    mustard

Bring the water, milk, and salt to a boil, reduce heat to simmer, and gradually pour in the potatoes, stirring constantly. Beat in remaining ingredients. Set aside until ready to use. Just before serving, place potatoes in a casserole and bake at 400° about 15 to 20 minutes.

Ahead of time: These can be prepared the day before or in the morning. Refrigerate, but bring to room temperature before final heating. Or, if hurried, heat the potato mixture directly from the refrigerator but allow more time in the oven.

Tip: These make an attractive garnish on planked steak, to embellish leftover lamb dishes, and in numerous other ways that will occur to you.

Always a Hit Twice-Baked Potatoes

[serves about 4]

2 large cold baked potatoes
    salt and pepper

3 tablespoons melted butter

Butter a shallow casserole. Peel and grate the potatoes and place them in the casserole, seasoning with salt and pepper. Spoon the melted butter over them. Bake, uncovered, at 400° for about 45 to 50 minutes, or until very well browned.

Ahead of time: This dish is best if prepared from potatoes baked the day before and chilled overnight. The dish can be assembled the day before and kept covered in the refrigerator. Bake just before serving.

Tip: These are so good and so easy to do that it is worth baking a double quantity of potatoes just for this purpose. And they are easy to prepare for a party.

A Party Spinach Casserole

[serves about 8]

2 (10-ounce) packages   ¾ to 1 teaspoon salt
     frozen chopped spinach   ¼ teaspoon pepper
¼ cup butter
8 ounces cream cheese,
     cubed

for the crumb topping
¾ cup dry bread crumbs   ¼ teaspoon salt
     (commercial are fine)   ¼ teaspoon nutmeg
¼ cup melted butter

Combine the ingredients for the topping and set aside. Defrost the spinach and drain it very well. Combine the spinach with the butter in a skillet and stir over moderate heat for 1 minute. Add the cream cheese, salt, and pepper and stir over low heat until it is mixed in. Place in a casserole and top with the crumb mixture. Bake in a 350° oven, uncovered, for about 20 to 30 minutes.

Ahead of time: Crumb topping can be mixed the day before.

Vegetable Casserole Sorcery

[serves about 10]

5 to 7 zucchini, peeled and
 sliced
2 cups cooked peas (canned
 petits pois or fresh or
 frozen peas)
½ pound fresh mushrooms,
 sautéed in butter, or
 canned mushrooms

1 (10½-ounce) can
 condensed cream of
 mushroom soup
1½ cups salted Mexican
 pumpkin seeds (or
 sliced salted nuts)

In a large casserole place a layer of sliced raw zucchini, next a layer of peas, then a layer of mushrooms. Spread with some of the soup. Repeat layers until all the vegetables have been used, ending with a layer of soup. Cover and bake at 350° for 30 minutes. Do not add additional liquid; the zucchini provides plenty of moisture when cooked. Remove from oven and cover the top thickly with the pumpkin seeds or nuts. Return to oven, uncovered, for another 15 minutes.

Ahead of time: This can be done up to the final baking the day before or in the morning or can be frozen at this stage. Bake with the pumpkin seeds or nuts just before serving.

An Auspicious Zucchini, Tomato, and Onion Casserole

[serves about 6]

6 medium-sized zucchini,
 peeled or unpeeled,
 sliced
3 fresh tomatoes, peeled
 and sliced (or 3 large
 canned tomatoes,
 sliced, and a tiny bit of
 juice)

1 small onion, peeled and
 finely sliced
 salt and pepper
2 tablespoons butter

Layer the zucchini, tomatoes, and onion in a casserole and season with salt and pepper. Dot with butter. Bake at 350°, uncovered, for about 1 hour.

Ahead of time: This can be made in the morning or the day before, or it can be frozen. It even seems to improve with reheating.

Zucchini with Corn

[serves 4 to 6]

5 medium-sized zucchini
salt and pepper
1¼ cups canned white or
yellow whole-kernel
corn

¼ teaspoon salt
½ cup sour cream
strips of swiss cheese

Cook the zucchini in simmering water for 4 to 5 minutes. Drain and cool. Cut in half lengthwise, scoop out seeds, and drain well (upside down) on paper towels. Place in a greased shallow casserole and season with salt and pepper. Combine the corn, ¼ teaspoon salt, and the sour cream, and fill the zucchini halves. Top with strips of cheese. Bake at 350° for 15 to 20 minutes.

Ahead of time: This can be assembled the day before or in the morning. Cover and refrigerate. Bring to room temperature before baking.

Unhurried Zucchini

[serves about 8 or more]

8 medium-sized zucchini
salt and pepper

1 cup sour cream
strips of well-aged
cheddar cheese

Cook the zucchini in simmering water for 4 to 5 minutes. Drain and cool. Cut in half lengthwise, scoop out seeds, and drain well upside down on paper towels. Place in a greased large shallow casserole and season with salt and pepper. Fill the cavities with the sour cream and top with strips of cheese. Bake at 350° for about 15 minutes. If browner tops are desired, run the zucchini under the broiling unit for a minute.

Ahead of time: This can be assembled the day before, then covered and refrigerated. Bring to room temperature before baking, or bake longer.

Zucchini Quickly Sautéed

[serves 4]

5 or 6 small zucchini   salt and pepper
2 tablespoons salad oil

Clean the zucchini but do not peel. Cut in ¼-inch-thick slices. Heat the oil in a skillet to sizzling. Add zucchini and toss and cook quickly—about 1 minute. Add salt and pepper to taste. Serve in a heated casserole.

Ahead of time: The zucchini can be sliced in the morning and kept in a plastic bag in the refrigerator. It is best to bring it to room temperature 1 or 2 hours before cooking.

≡Easiest

Deliciously Baked Cauliflower

[serves about 4]

1 medium-sized cauliflower,
  separated into bite-sized
  flowerets
salt and pepper
1 (10½-ounce) can
  condensed cream of
  celery soup
2 tablespoons milk
2 tablespoons madeira or
  sherry
¾ cup grated cheddar
  cheese

Place the cauliflower in a shallow casserole and season with salt and pepper. Combine the remaining ingredients and spoon over cauliflower. Cover with foil, and bake about 40 minutes in a 350° oven, then uncover and bake another 5 minutes.

Celery with Onion and Dill

[serves about 4]

3 cups sliced celery
4 green onions, chopped
½ cup freshly chopped dill
  (see "Frosted" Herbs,
  Handy Dandy No. 6,
  p. 6)
¼ cup butter
salt and pepper

Place all the ingredients in a saucepan and stir over high heat for 1 minute. Cover and lower heat to simmer. Cook 1 or 2 more minutes. Celery should remain crisp.

Ahead of time: The celery and onions can be sliced in the morning. Keep refrigerated in a plastic bag. Bring to room temperature an hour or so before cooking.

Celery Sauté

[serves about 6]

4 cups sliced celery (about ¼-inch thick)

2 tablespoons oil
2 tablespoons soy sauce

Sauté (stir and fry) the celery in the oil over high heat for about 2 minutes. Add the soy sauce and stir-fry another minute. Celery should remain very crisp.

Ahead of time: The celery can be sliced in the morning and kept refrigerated in a plastic bag.

Two Super Easy Corn Casseroles

[serves about 6]

I. WITH JACK CHEESE

1 (17-ounce) can creamed corn
⅔ cup heavy cream
¼ cup yellow cornmeal
1 (4-ounce) can green chiles, seeded and chopped

1 teaspoon salt
¼ pound jack cheese, coarsely grated or diced
3 eggs, beaten

Combine all ingredients. Pour into a casserole. Bake at 350° for about 40 to 45 minutes.

Ahead of time: Reheats beautifully next day—maybe tastes even better. It freezes well too.

II. WITH CHEDDAR CHEESE

1 (17-ounce) can creamed
   corn
1 cup sour cream
¾ teaspoon salt
1 teaspoon baking soda
1 tablespoon sugar
1 (4-ounce) can green
   chiles, seeded and
   chopped

¼ cup yellow cornmeal
¼ pound cheddar cheese,
   grated or diced
3 eggs, beaten

Combine all ingredients. Pour into a casserole. Bake at 350° for about 40 to 45 minutes.

Ahead of time: This too reheats beautifully the next day. It can be frozen.

Tip: Both of these are great. For an even more delicious corn casserole, which takes a little more effort, see *Superlative Corn and Green Chile Casserole*, p. 152.

Freedom Mushrooms

[serves about 6]

1 pound fresh mushrooms,
   cleaned
½ cup melted butter
½ cup boiling water
2 chicken bouillon cubes
   (Knorr's if possible)

½ teaspoon thyme
2 tablespoons chopped
   green onions

Place the mushrooms in a casserole. Pour the butter over them and stir. Combine the remaining ingredients and pour over mushrooms. Cover and bake at 325° for 1 hour.

Tip: These are good served with just about anything from steak to chicken to hamburgers.

Mushrooms Easily Delicious˘

[serves 10 to 12]

24 to 36 giant fresh
    mushrooms
1 cup melted butter (or
    more if needed)

salt and pepper

Clean the mushrooms and dry thoroughly. Dip each mushroom in melted butter, then place in a baking-serving dish and season with salt and pepper. Don't crowd them; if necessary use more than one dish. Bake in a 400° oven for 10 to 15 minutes. The mushrooms should remain somewhat firm, so do not overcook.

Ahead of time: The mushrooms can be dipped in butter and arranged in their baking dish in the morning. Leave at room temperature, lightly covered. Bake just before serving.

Potatoes Simple Simon

[serves about 4]

1 (12-ounce) package frozen
    shredded potatoes,
    defrosted

salt and pepper
1 cup heavy cream

Place the potatoes in a shallow casserole. Season. Cover with the cream and bake (uncovered) in the topmost part of the oven at 350° for about 60 minutes. If desired, brown the top for a minute or two under the broiling unit.

Tip: This can be doubled or tripled, but do not bake in too thick a layer; use two casseroles if necessary.

Funny but Yummy Potatoes

[serves about 6]

1 package instant mashed
  potatoes (French's)
1 (1-pound) can of
  sauerkraut, very well
  drained (squeeze if
  necessary)

1 cup shredded cheddar
  cheese

Prepare the potatoes as directed on the package. Combine with the sauerkraut and half the cheese and place in a casserole. Top with remaining cheese and bake (uncovered) for about 30 minutes.

Ahead of time: This can be combined the day before or in the morning; it reheats well too.

New Potatoes, Easily Roasted

small, uniform new potatoes
salad oil
salt

Peel the potatoes, rinse, and dry. Coat thoroughly with salad oil and place in a shallow pan large enough that potatoes do not touch. Sprinkle with salt. Place in a 400° oven and roast for about 1 hour or until done and well browned.

Tip: These are especially good with *Top Sirloin Steak Baked*, p. 128.

Contemporary Potatoes Boulangère

[serves about 6]

5 medium-sized boiling potatoes, sliced about ⅛- to ¼-inch thick	1½ to 2 cups beef bouillon (canned is fine)
1 large onion, thinly sliced	salt and pepper

Place a layer of potatoes in a casserole, then a layer of onion; continue layering until all potato and onion slices have been used, seasoning each layer with salt and pepper. Pour the bouillon over all and bake in a 350° oven (uncovered) for 1½ to 2 hours, or until potatoes are done and top is well browned.

Ahead of time: This lends itself especially well to before-the-event cooking. It can be cooked as much as two days before (or months before and frozen) because it reheats beautifully.

Tip: If you can find only baking potatoes, slice them thicker since they tend to fall apart rather easily.

Baked Cherry Tomatoes

[serves about 12]

3 baskets of cherry tomatoes (about 6 cups)	½ cup melted butter
	salt and pepper

Be sure the tomatoes are at room temperature. Remove stems and place tomatoes in a baking dish that you can serve from. Pour the butter over the tomatoes, season with salt and pepper, toss lightly, and just before serving place in a 400° oven for about 5 minutes. These do not need to cook; they just need heating through.

Ahead of time: These can be assembled in the morning and left at room temperature ready to bake later.

Baked Tomatoes with Onion

firm tomatoes, cut in half   thin whole slices of onion
salt and pepper   butter
prepared mustard

Place the tomatoes in a baking pan, cut side up. Sprinkle with salt and pepper. Spread with mustard, then place a slice of onion on each tomato half. Dot with butter. Bake at 350° for 15 to 20 minutes.

Ahead of time: These can be assembled in the morning and refrigerated. Bake shortly before serving.

Ruth Benson's Restful Zucchini

zucchini   salt and pepper
Garlic Oil, Handy Dandy. No. 1, grated parmesan cheese
  p. 3   melted butter

Wash zucchini and cut off ends, then slice each in half lengthwise. Brush with *Garlic Oil* and place in a baking pan. Season with salt and pepper. Sprinkle with parmesan and with melted butter. Bake 20 to 25 minutes (uncovered) in a 375° oven.

Ahead of time: These can be assembled in the morning. Cover and leave at room temperature until time to bake.

9/SALADS

Easy

Asparagus Salad Deluxe

[serves 10 to 12]

6 pounds fresh asparagus
salt and pepper
*In the Manner of
Hollandaise, Handy
Dandy No. 4, p. 4 (but
do not heat)*

1 cup canned pimento,
drained and cut in
strips
½ cup chopped green
onions
¼ cup chopped parsley

Cook the asparagus until barely tender. Drain and chill. Arrange on a large platter or on individual plates. Spoon the sauce over tips. Decorate sauce-covered tips with the pimento strips, chopped green onions, and parsley. Serve very cold.

Ahead of time: Asparagus can be cooked the day before and kept refrigerated, as can the sauce. Add the sauce and garnish shortly before serving.

Tip: This makes an excellent first course at a dinner party.

Green Salad with Bacon and Eggs

[serves about 6 to 8]

1 head romaine lettuce plus
enough other salad
greens (spinach or
whatever) to serve 6 to
8
¾ cup chopped green
onions

4 hard-boiled eggs, sliced
⅓ pound sliced bacon,
cooked crisp, then
crumbled

for the dressing

1 teaspoon salt
½ teaspoon pepper
¼ teaspoon paprika
¾ teaspoon dry mustard
2 tablespoons sugar

¼ cup lemon juice
2 tablespoons vinegar
½ cup bacon fat (left from
cooking bacon)

Arrange the romaine and other greens in a large salad bowl. Sprinkle with the green onions and sliced eggs. Combine the dressing ingredients in a small saucepan and stir over low heat. Do not boil. Sprinkle the crumbled bacon over the salad. Add the dressing, toss, and serve at once.

Ahead of time: The greens, onions, and eggs can be arranged in a bowl in the morning, covered, and refrigerated until time to serve. Cook and crumble the bacon, warm the dressing, and add just before serving.

Tip: Please note: this should be eaten at once after dressing has been added.

Gazpacho Salad

[serves about 8]

2 cucumbers, peeled, quartered lengthwise, then sliced
1 box cherry tomatoes, halved
1 green pepper, chopped
2 cups thinly sliced celery
2 cups sliced radishes
5 green onions, chopped
1¼ cups sliced artichoke bottoms (canned are fine)

1 tablespoon chopped parsley
salt and pepper to taste
French Dressing, Handy Dandy No. 7, p. 7
1 avocado, diced (optional)
watercress to garnish

Combine all the vegetables (except the avocado and watercress) with salt and pepper to taste and the dressing. Cover and chill. Shortly before serving, add avocado (if used). Serve in small chilled bowls; garnish with watercress.

Ahead of time: Except for the avocado and watercress the salad can be combined the day before or in the morning. Keep covered and refrigerated.

Spinach Salad with Piñon Nuts, Eggs, and Bacon

[serves about 8 to 10]

1 pound fresh spinach,
   cleaned, stems
   discarded
6 hard-boiled eggs
4 green onions, chopped
½ cup toasted piñon nuts
   (or toasted slivered
   almonds)

¼ to ½ pound sliced bacon,
   cooked and crumbled
French Dressing, Handy
   Dandy No. 7, p. 7

Tear the spinach leaves into bite-sized pieces and place in a large salad bowl. Slice the eggs and distribute over top and sides. Sprinkle with the green onions, piñon nuts, and crumbled bacon. Add the dressing, toss, and serve.

Ahead of time: The spinach and other ingredients (except the bacon) can be placed in a bowl in the morning, covered tightly with plastic wrap, and kept refrigerated. Prepare the bacon and add it and the dressing just before serving.

Spinach Salad with Raisins and Piñon Nuts

[serves 4]

1 red onion, thinly sliced
½ pound fresh spinach,
   washed and dried,
   stems and heavy veins
   removed
½ cup raisins, washed in
   very hot water, then
   drained and dried

½ cup piñon nuts, toasted in
   the oven (or slivered
   almonds, chopped
   walnuts, or other nuts)
French Dressing, Handy
   Dandy No. 7, p. 7

Place the sliced onion in the bottom of a salad bowl. Top with the spinach. Scatter the raisins and nuts over the top. Add dressing to taste and toss.

Ahead of time: The salad can be arranged in the bowl, covered, and kept chilled from early morning on. Add the dressing just before serving.

Walter Horn's Salad of Dandelion Greens

[serves 6 to 8]

1 large bunch dandelion
   greens
4 green onions, chopped

3 or more ripe tomatoes,
   cut in small wedges
*French Dressing, Handy
   Dandy No. 7,* p. 7

Wash the greens thoroughly, then drain and dry them. Cut in any desired length and place in a salad bowl. Sprinkle with the green onions and scatter the tomato wedges over the salad. Add dressing, toss, and serve.

Ahead of time: The salad can be completely arranged in a bowl, covered tightly with plastic wrap, and refrigerated in the morning. Toss with dressing just before serving.

Tip: Dandelion greens used to be gathered in the fields; improved varieties are now cultivated, but you may have to look for them in specialty markets. These tantalizing, slightly bitter greens are well worth the search.

Corn, Carrot, Chile, and Olive Salad
For Avocados or Tomatoes

[serves about 12]

3 (12-ounce) cans whole-
   kernel corn, drained
1 (2½-ounce) can ripe olives
   (or more if you prefer),
   drained and sliced
1 onion, chopped
1 (7-ounce) can green
   chiles, seeded and
   chopped

1 cup chopped raw carrots
6 large ripe avocados or 12
   medium-sized ripe
   tomatoes
chopped fresh parsley (for
   later garnishing)

for the dressing
1 cup sugar
2 cups vinegar
½ cup salad oil (not olive
   oil)
1 clove garlic, mashed, or
   garlic from *Garlic Oil,
   Handy Dandy, No. 1*, p.
   3

3 teaspoons salt
½ teaspoon pepper

To make the dressing, heat the sugar and vinegar together only until sugar has dissolved, then combine with other dressing ingredients. Place all other ingredients except avocados or tomatoes and parsley in a bowl and add the dressing. Cover and chill at least 24 hours. Drain before using. Fill avocado halves or hollow out the tomatoes and fill. Garnish the tops with parsley.

Ahead of time: This must be made at least a day in advance. It will keep for weeks in the refrigerator.

Tip: Instead of filling avocados or tomatoes, this salad can be served from a bowl—especially nice at a buffet.

Swiss Cheese and Egg Salad

[serves 8 to 12]

14 hard-boiled eggs
1 pound imported swiss
   cheese, cut into sticks
   about 1 inch long and
   ¼ inch thick
salt and pepper to taste

1 cup sour cream
1 teaspoon dry mustard
1 cup Durkee's Dressing
   paprika
   chopped parsley

Set aside 2 eggs for the garnish. Chop the remaining eggs and combine with the cheese, salt, pepper, sour cream, mustard, and Durkee's. Taste for seasoning; you may want to add more Durkee's. Spoon into an attractive bowl or onto a platter. Sieve the yolks of the reserved eggs and chop the whites. Decorate the top of the salad by sprinkling alternating rows of egg yolk, whites, paprika, and parsley. Cover with plastic wrap and chill until time to serve.

Ahead of time: This can be made the day before. Keep well covered and refrigerated.

Tip: This has eye appeal and a marvelous taste. Especially useful for a buffet supper, but the recipe can be easily cut in half or thirds for smaller gatherings.

Ma Maison Potato Salad

[serves 6 to 8]

2 extra-large or 3 medium-
   sized cooked potatoes
6 hard-boiled eggs, sliced
3 green onions, chopped
3 tablespoons chopped
   sweet pickle

1 red or green sweet
   pepper, chopped
1 cup sour cream
1 tablespoon vinegar
½ cup Durkee's Dressing
   salt and pepper

Combine all ingredients, taste for seasoning, then chill.

Ahead of time: This can be made the day before or earlier. It should keep several days in the refrigerator.

Tip: This can be mixed with mayonnaise, omitting the sour cream and Durkee's; you may want to eliminate the vinegar.

Apple, Pear, Ginger, Grape, and Raisin Salad

sliced peeled apples
sliced peeled pears
raisins soaked in a little sherry
fresh grapes, cut in half and
  seeded

chopped candied ginger
a little orange juice or lemon
  juice
a little whipped cream (or
  mayonnaise)

Mix all together to your taste. Chill and serve.

Ahead of time: This can be assembled in the morning. Cover and chill until time to serve.

Tip: This salad evolved from what happened to be on hand one day; it can consist of any combination of the listed ingredients, and part of the fun is trying it in varying proportions. You do need the orange juice or lemon juice to reduce the darkening of the apples and pears. It is a good, sweet, crunchy salad, delicious with baked ham or poultry.

Honeydew Melon with a Curried Apple-Celery-Almond Salad

[serves 4 to 6]

1½ cups diced apple
1½ cups chopped celery
2 tablespoons lemon juice
1½ teaspoons curry powder
⅛ teaspoon salt
½ cup mayonnaise
⅓ cup sliced toasted
    almonds

4 to 6 slices honeydew
    melon, cut ½ inch thick
    and full circle, then
    seeds and rind removed
chutney
additional toasted sliced
    almonds to garnish
    (optional)

Combine the apple, celery, lemon juice, curry powder, salt, mayonnaise, and the ⅓ cup almonds. Place the melon rounds on individual plates (or arrange on a very large platter). Fill the centers with the salad. Place a spoonful of chutney on top of each in the center, and, if desired, sprinkle all with additional almonds.

Ahead of time: The apple-celery mixture can be prepared the day before or in the morning, covered, and kept refrigerated. Stir well before using.

Nonesuch Fruit Salad for Spicy Occasions

[serves about 10]

5 large bananas, each cut in 4 chunks
2 cups sour cream
2 cups shredded or flaked coconut (canned is fine)

1 fresh pineapple, cut in thick slices
fresh grapes, raspberries, or strawberries
lettuce (Bibb or other)

Spread the banana chunks thickly with sour cream, then roll them in the coconut. Both the sour cream and coconut coatings should be very generous. Arrange all the fruit on lettuce (either on one giant platter or on individual plates) and serve very cold.

Ahead of time: The fruit can be readied in the morning, including the coating of the banana chunks. Chill each fruit separately. Arrange shortly before serving.

Tip: A sumptuous yet cooling accompaniment to hot, spicy curries and to dishes such as the *Indonesian Chicken* (p. 88) or *Indonesian Lamb* (p. 124). Don't hesitate to substitute different kinds of fruit (sliced oranges for pineapple, for example), but the coated bananas are a must.

Easier

Alberta Horn's Moyashi Sunomono (Salad of Fresh Bean Sprouts)

[serves 6 to 8]

1 pound fresh bean sprouts

2 fresh carrots, peeled and shredded

for the dressing

2 tablespoons salad oil

1 tablespoon white sesame seeds

6 tablespoons sugar

½ cup rice vinegar (or white wine vinegar)

½ teaspoon salt

Place the bean sprouts and shredded carrots in a large bowl. Heat the oil in a saucepan and add the sesame seeds. Cook over moderate heat until seeds are light brown. Remove from heat and add the remaining ingredients. Stir until the sugar has dissolved, then pour over the bean sprouts and carrots. Toss well, then refrigerate at least for several hours.

Ahead of time: This can be made several days ahead and kept covered and refrigerated.

Sweet Pepper Salad with Watercress

[serves 8 to 10]

1 large green sweet pepper, thinly sliced

1 large red sweet pepper, thinly sliced

2 or 3 yellow sweet peppers, thinly sliced (if you can't find these, use more green or red peppers)

1 red onion, finely sliced

2 bunches watercress, washed and drained, then heavy stems removed

French Dressing, Handy Dandy No. 7, p. 7

Place the peppers, onion, and watercress in a large salad bowl. Cover and chill. Toss with the dressing just before serving.

204 /

Ahead of time: The vegetables can be cut and placed in the salad bowl in the early morning, covered tightly, and kept chilled. Do not add dressing until time to serve.

Green Knight Salad

[serves about 10]

2 heads romaine lettuce
2 cucumbers, peeled and
    thinly sliced
¼ cup chopped fresh dill
    (see *"Frosted" Herbs,*
    Dandy No. 6, p. 6)

1½ cups seedless green
    grapes

for the dressing
½ cup lemon juice
1 teaspoon salt
1 teaspoon sugar

¼ teaspoon pepper
1½ cups very mild olive oil
    (or other salad oil)

Combine the dressing ingredients and mix thoroughly. Chill until ready to use. Combine the salad ingredients in a bowl, add the dressing, toss, and serve.

Ahead of time: The salad can be arranged in a bowl, covered, and refrigerated in the morning. The dressing can be made several days ahead and chilled. Combine just before serving.

Family Cole Slaw Favorite

[serves about 8]

1 large solid green cabbage, shredded or finely sliced

1 green pepper, chopped
4 green onions, chopped

for the dressing

1½ cups mayonnaise (or part sour cream)
1 teaspoon salt
¼ teaspoon pepper

⅓ cup vinegar (or part lemon juice)
⅓ cup sugar

Combine the ingredients for the dressing and pour it over the vegetables. Mix well and chill for at least several hours.

Ahead of time: This can be made several days ahead of time, covered, and refrigerated. It .is best made at least 24 hours ahead.

String Bean Salad with Toasted Filberts

[serves about 6]

1 pound fresh string beans, sliced lengthwise
French Dressing, Handy Dandy No. 7, p. 7

lettuce
½ cup toasted filberts, grated or ground

Cook the string beans until tender but not mushy. Drain and cool slightly. Marinate in the dressing and chill several hours. Arrange the beans on lettuce on a platter or on individual plates and pour a little of the marinade over them. Cover tops generously with the nuts.

Ahead of time: This can be prepared the day before or in the morning; however, do not add nuts until just before serving.

Raw Mushroom Salad with Tarragon

[serves 4 to 8]

1 pound fresh mushrooms
juice of 1 lemon
¾ cup mayonnaise
salt to taste
3 teaspoons tomato paste

2 teaspoons chopped fresh
tarragon (or ¾ teaspoon
dried)
1 tablespoon madeira

Clean and slice the mushrooms and sprinkle with the lemon juice. Combine the remaining ingredients, add to mushrooms, and stir gently. Cover and chill; serve cold.

Ahead of time: This can be done the day before or in the morning. The dressing will separate, but do not worry—just stir it again and serve.

A Greek "Peasant" Salad

[serves 6 to 8]

2 green peppers, thinly
sliced
2 cucumbers, thinly sliced
1 or 2 red onions, thinly
sliced
2 bunches watercress,
washed and drained,
then heavy stems
removed

1 cup feta cheese, crumbled
1 cup pitted ripe olives
3 tomatoes, cut in small
wedges
*French Dressing, Handy
Dandy No. 7, p. 7*

Combine the green peppers, cucumbers, onions, and watercress in a large salad bowl. Scatter the cheese, olives, and tomato wedges over the top. Cover and chill. Toss with the dressing just before serving.

Ahead of time: The salad can be combined without the dressing in the morning, covered, and kept refrigerated until time to toss and serve.

Avocado Salad Vinaigrette

chopped cucumber
chopped tomato
chopped green onions
chopped green pepper

French Dressing, Handy Dandy
 Dandy No. 7, p. 7
salt and pepper
peeled avocado halves

Combine the chopped vegetables with the dressing and salt and pepper to taste. Chill, then use to fill avocado halves.

Ahead of time: The chopped vegetables can be combined with the dressing and kept refrigerated for two to three days. The avocado halves can be peeled and dipped in lemon juice in the morning (keep covered and cold); fill shortly before serving.

Endive and Grapefruit Salad

[serves 4]

4 Belgian endives, split
   lengthwise
1 large grapefruit,
   segmented

1 or 2 chopped green
   onions (optional)

for the dressing
¼ cup grapefruit juice
½ teaspoon salt
¼ teaspoon pepper

2 teaspoons sugar
½ teaspoon dry mustard
½ cup salad oil

Make the salad dressing: Combine grapefruit juice with salt, pepper, sugar, and mustard and beat with a whisk, then beat in the oil. Set aside (or chill) until time to serve. Place 1 split endive on each individual plate. Divide the grapefruit on top of the endive and pour dressing over each. Top with a sprinkling of green onions if desired.

Ahead of time: The dressing and the grapefruit segments can be prepared the day before and kept refrigerated.

Romaine and Orange Salad

[serves about 10]

1 very large head romaine
lettuce (or two small
ones)
1 cup sliced pitted black
olives
4 navel oranges, sectioned
2 green peppers, sliced in
thin strips

4 green onions, chopped
1 head watercress, washed,
dried, and heavy stems
removed
*French Dressing, Handy
Dandy No. 7, p. 7*

Combine all salad ingredients, add dressing to taste, then toss
and serve.

Ahead of time: The salad can be combined in the morning, covered tightly with plastic, and kept chilled until time to serve.
Toss with the dressing just before ready to eat.

Easiest

Bean Sprout and Tomato Salad

[serves 8 to 10]

2 quarts fresh bean sprouts
2 cups halved cherry
tomatoes (or the
equivalent in pieces or
wedges from regular
tomatoes)

6 green onions, chopped
French Dressing, Handy
Dandy No. 7, p. 7

Combine the bean sprouts, tomatoes, and green onions in a large salad bowl. Add dressing to taste, toss, and serve.

Ahead of time: The vegetables can be kept covered and chilled from the morning on, until time to serve; add dressing and toss just before serving.

Walnut Salad

[serves about 6]

1 large head romaine lettuce
1½ cups very thinly sliced
celery

1½ cups walnuts, coarsely
chopped, lightly toasted
in a 300° oven

for the dressing

1½ teaspoons salt
¼ teaspoon pepper
1 teaspoon sugar
½ teaspoon dry mustard
⅓ cup lemon juice

1 cup salad oil (if possible
imported French walnut
oil, or else a very bland
olive oil)

Combine the romaine and celery in a salad bowl. Scatter with toasted walnuts. Combine the dressing ingredients, add desired amount, toss, and serve.

Ahead of time: The romaine and celery can be placed in a salad bowl in the morning, covered with plastic wrap, and chilled. Add the walnuts and dressing just before serving.

Celery and Sweet Peppers with Mustard Dressing

[serves 2 to 4]

2 cups thinly sliced celery	¼ cup Dijon-style mustard
1 cup thinly sliced red or green sweet peppers	2 tablespoons heavy cream
	salt and pepper to taste

Mix all ingredients together and chill. Serve very cold as is, or arrange on lettuce leaves.

Ahead of time: This can be prepared in the morning.

Raw Vegetable Platter

red cabbage, cut in wedges	celery sticks
tomatoes, cut in wedges	green onions
green pepper, cut in ½-inch long slices	

Arrange the vegetables decoratively on a large platter. Serve with something like *Beef Fondue*, p. 118.

Ahead of time: This can be readied the day before; keep cut vegetables refrigerated in plastic bags. Or the platter can be arranged in the morning, covered tightly with plastic or foil, and kept refrigerated until time to serve.

Carrot Salad

[serves 4 to 6]

3 cups grated fresh carrots (pack to measure)
¼ cup orange juice
2 teaspoons lemon juice

½ cup raisins, washed in hot water, then drained
¾ cup mayonnaise

Combine all thoroughly. Cover and chill for at least several hours—better overnight.

Ahead of time: This can be prepared several days ahead and kept refrigerated.

Cucumbers Scandinavian Style

¼ teaspoon salt
½ cup vinegar
¼ cup water

¼ cup sugar
2 large cucumbers, peeled and thinly sliced

Mix the salt, vinegar, water, and sugar together. Add the cucumbers, stir, and press down. Cover and chill. When ready to serve, drain and serve cold.

Ahead of time: These can be prepared several days ahead and refrigerated; they should be done at least 24 hours ahead for best flavor.

Tip: As a nice extra, try adding either some chopped fresh parsley or some chopped fresh dill.

Endive Salad with Olives, Beets, and Eggs

Belgian endives, cut in
quarters lengthwise

sliced pickled beets (canned
are fine)

chopped hard-boiled eggs

chopped ripe olives (canned
are fine)

*French Dressing,Handy Dandy
No. 7*, p. 7

Use 1 endive per guest. Place the quartered endives on a large platter (for a buffet), or place 1 on each individual serving plate. Sprinkle beets, eggs, and olives over the endives and spoon on *French Dressing*. Serve chilled.

Ahead of time: The endives can be arranged with the beets, eggs, and olives in the morning; cover tightly and keep refrigerated. Add dressing just before serving.

Super-Easy Turkey Salad

[serves about 6]

4 cups diced cooked turkey

1½ cups chopped celery

1½ cups mayonnaise (about)

salt and pepper to taste

1 tablespoon soy sauce

1 teaspoon curry powder

to garnish

1 or 2 cups well-drained
pineapple chunks

⅔ cup sliced almonds,
toasted

Combine the salad ingredients and chill. Just before serving, cover the top of the salad with the pineapple chunks and scatter with the toasted almonds.

Ahead of time: This can be prepared the day before or in the morning. Garnish just before serving.

Tip: This makes an elegant luncheon dish served in individual bowls or dishes on red lettuce or Bibb lettuce and accompanied with a delicious hot bread.

Niçoise for Four

[serves 4 for luncheon or 8 as a first course for dinner]

2 (7-ounce) cans tunafish in
oil, drained and broken
into largish pieces
2 green sweet peppers, cut
in chunks or slices
3 small tomatoes, cut in
wedges

*French Dressing, Handy
Dandy No. 7, p. 7*
lettuce
12 anchovies
12 ripe olives
4 hard-boiled eggs, cut in
wedges

Combine the tunafish, peppers, and tomatoes with the dressing (to your taste). Divide on lettuce-lined plates (or in bowls). Garnish tops with the anchovies, olives, and egg wedges.

Ahead of time: The eggs can be cooked the day before and the vegetables can be cut in the morning.

Tip: Besides being an ideal luncheon dish, this can be a super first course at dinner; for that purpose, use this amount for 8 guests.

2 Skewered Fruit Arrangements

VARIATION I

*Ported Prunes, Handy Dandy No.
22, p. 18*

watermelon pickles
preserved kumquats

Pit the prunes. Place a prune, a watermelon pickle, and a kumquat on each skewer (metal or bamboo).

VARIATION II

large fresh pineapple cubes
orange chunks
banana chunks,
    dipped in lemon juice

cantaloupe cubes
large strawberries
fresh figs, peeled

Arrange your choice of fruits on skewers (metal or bamboo) and chill until needed.

Ahead of time: Both variations can be assembled in the morning. Both should be kept covered, but Variation II should be refrigerated.

Tip: Both variations can be served on individual plates (lined with lettuce if you like) or on large platters (for buffets), and both are good company for roast lamb, beef, poultry, or ham; good too with curries.

Lichi Nuts with Cream Cheese and Ginger

[makes about 24; serves 8 to 12]

2 (3-ounce) packages cream
   cheese
2 tablespoons cognac
4 tablespoons candied
   ginger, chopped

1 (20-ounce) can lichi nuts,
   well drained
lettuce

Combine the cream cheese, cognac, and ginger. Fill the lichi nuts with this mixture and chill. Serve on any kind of lettuce on small salad plates—2 or 3 stuffed lichis per guest.

Ahead of time: The cream-cheese mixture can be prepared the day before. The lichi nuts can be stuffed in the morning.

Tip: These are especially good served with meat or poultry done in a teriyaki style (as in recipes on pp. 103, 133).

10/BREADS, ROLLS, AND COFFEE CAKES

Easy

Baking Powder Biscuits Two Ways

[makes about 12]

I. FROM SCRATCH

2 cups sifted flour	⅓ cup vegetable shortening
1 teaspoon salt	⅔ cup milk
3 teaspoons baking powder	

Sift the dry ingredients together. Cut in the shortening with two knives or with a pastry blender. Stir in the milk. Turn out on a floured board and knead for about ½ minute—just until smooth. Pat or roll into a circle about ¾-inch thick. Cut to desired size (I use a round cutter 1½ inches in diameter). Bake at 450° for 12 to 15 minutes.

II. FROM HOMEMADE BISCUIT MIX

2 cups *Homemade Biscuit Mix, Handy Dandy No. 14*, p. 12	⅔ cup milk

Follow directions above.

Ahead of time: Biscuits by either recipe can be prepared in the morning. Keep refrigerated until time to bake. If cold, the baking time may need to be a few minutes longer.

Banana Caramel Biscuits

[makes about 12]

2 cups *Homemade Biscuit Mix, Handy Dandy No. 14*, p. 12	½ cup melted butter
	brown sugar
	cinnamon
2 ripe bananas, mashed	

Mix biscuit mix and the mashed bananas together. Knead, then roll into a rectangle. Spread with some of the melted butter and sprinkle generously with brown sugar and cinnamon. Roll up jelly-roll fashion and cut into about 12 portions. Put a generous teaspoon of melted butter in each of 12 muffin tins and top each with a generous teaspoon of brown sugar. Place a piece of dough (cut side down) in each tin. Bake at 450° for 12 to 15 minutes. Turn out upside down immediately and serve hot.

Ahead of time: These can be prepared up to the point of baking either in the morning or the day before. Keep refrigerated and bake a little longer. They can also be reheated after baking.

Enchantment Walnut Rolls

[makes about 2 dozen]

2 cups walnuts, lightly toasted and then chopped into medium-sized pieces

1¼ cups butter, softened extra-thin sliced whole-wheat bread (Pepperidge Farm if possible)

Make a walnut butter by combining the toasted chopped walnuts with the butter. Flatten the bread slices with a rolling pin (it is not necessary to remove the crusts). Spread the walnut-butter mixture generously on the slices, then roll them up diagonally and place on cookie sheets. Bake at 400° for about 15 to 20 minutes—until lightly browned and nicely crisp.

Ahead of time: The walnut butter can be made several days ahead, covered, and kept refrigerated. The rolls can be prepared in the morning, covered with plastic wrap, and left at room temperature. Bake just before serving.

Tip: These have an amazing appeal. Whether they are served with a first course of salad or soup or by themselves as an appetizer, there never seem to be enough.

Quick Coffee Cake Ace of Spades

⅓ cup butter
¾ cup sugar
1 egg
½ cup milk
1½ cups sifted flour

2 teaspoons baking powder
½ teaspoon salt
⅓ cup apricot jam·
¼ cup currant jelly (or
    strawberry jam)

for the topping
¼ cup brown sugar
1 teaspoon cinnamon

3 tablespoons melted butter
½ cup chopped nuts

Cream the butter and sugar together, then beat in the egg. Sift the dry ingredients together, then add alternately with the milk, using only a few strokes. Do not beat. Pour into a greased and floured 8-inch-square pan. Dot with apricot jam and currant jelly or strawberry jam. Combine the topping ingredients and sprinkle the mixture over the dough. Bake at 350° for 25 to 35 minutes. Serve hot or warm.

Ahead of time: This can be baked in the morning or the day before or can be frozen after baking. Reheat before serving.

Daniel's Favorite Banana Pancakes

3 eggs
1 cup sifted flour
½ teaspoon baking soda
¼ teaspoon salt

1¼ cups warm milk
¼ cup melted butter
1 mashed banana

Beat the eggs, then add the flour (mixed with the soda and salt) alternately with the milk. Add the melted butter and the banana. Let stand about 15 minutes. Add more milk if batter is too thick. Cook in a skillet (or on a griddle) in plenty of butter. I make them small—about 3 inches across—and serve with maple or boysenberry syrup.

Ahead of time: These can be cooked, stacked with melted butter between pancakes, and covered with foil, then later reheated in the oven. They can even be done the day before and refrigerated, and they can be frozen. Bring to room temperature, then reheat in foil packets in a 300° oven. Be sure there is ample melted butter between the pancakes; if needed, brush more melted butter on each as they are reheated.

Whole-Wheat Banana Bread with Grand Marnier

[one 3 × 5 × 9 loaf]

½ cup butter at room
    temperature
1 cup sugar
2 extra-large eggs
¼ teaspoon salt
1 teaspoon baking powder
2 cups whole-wheat flour
    (measure by spooning
    into a cup, then level
    with a knife)

2 tablespoons strong coffee
2 tablespoons Grand
    Marnier
1 cup mashed ripe bananas
    (about 3)

Cream the butter and sugar until fluffy. Beat in the eggs. Mix dry ingredients together and add alternately with the coffee, Grand Marnier, and bananas. Bake in a well-greased and floured bread-loaf pan (3 × 5 × 9) at 350° for 30 minutes. Reduce heat to 325° or 300° and bake until loaf tests done (when a toothpick inserted comes out clean). Remove from pan and cool on a rack.

Ahead of time: This can be baked the day before. Keep well wrapped in double foil. It can be frozen; defrost and bring to room temperature before serving.

Pumpkin Spice Bread Easily Made

[makes 2 8-inch loaves or 4 smaller loaves]

2 cups sugar
1 cup brown sugar (pack to measure)
1 (1-pound) can pumpkin (2 cups)
1 cup vegetable oil
4 eggs
4 cups sifted flour (17 ounces)
2 teaspoons baking soda

1 teaspoon salt
2 teaspoons nutmeg
2 teaspoons cinnamon
1 teaspoon ginger
½ teaspoon powdered cloves
⅓ cup water
1 cup chopped walnuts
2 cups raisins, soaked in hot water, then drained

Combine the sugars, pumpkin, oil, and eggs in a bowl and beat until blended. Combine the dry ingredients and mix well (or sift together several times) and add to pumpkin mixture. Add the water, nuts, and raisins; stir. Spoon the dough into greased and floured pans. Bake at 350° for 60 to 85 minutes, depending on size of pans. (Watch that tops do not burn; reduce temperature to 300° if necessary.) Remove and cool in pans on racks for about 15 minutes, then turn breads out and finish cooling. Serve hot or slightly warm.

Ahead of time: These can be baked several days ahead and they freeze well too. Bring to room temperature, wrap in foil, and re-heat in a 325° oven before serving.

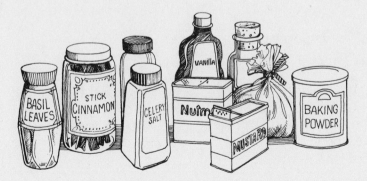

Easier

Margaret Hall's Failsafe Popovers

[makes about 6]

1 cup sifted flour
¾ teaspoon salt
1 cup milk (at room
   temperature)

2 large eggs, slightly beaten
1 teaspoon melted butter or
   oil

Combine the flour and salt in a bowl. Combine the milk, eggs, and oil, then gradually add to the flour, stirring until well mixed. Grease cold custard cups with vegetable shortening and fill them about half full of batter. Place them on a baking sheet and place in a *cold oven*—yes, I mean a cold oven. Immediately turn oven to 400° and bake 45 to 60 minutes, depending on how cold the batter is.

Ahead of time: The batter can be made the day before, covered, and refrigerated, or made several hours before baking and left covered at room temperature. When batter stands, it may be advisable to stir in a few more tablespoons of milk before baking, since it thickens somewhat.

Tip: Since these are so easy you may want to make more; the recipe can easily be doubled.

Pseudo-Doughnuts

[makes 12]

1¾ cups sifted flour
¾ cup sugar
2 teaspoons baking powder
½ teaspoon salt
½ teaspoon nutmeg

⅓ cup melted butter or oil
½ cup milk
1 teaspoon vanilla
1 egg

for after baking
½ cup unsalted (sweet)
   butter, melted

1 cup sugar combined with
   1 tablespoon (or more)
   cinnamon

Sift the flour, sugar, baking powder, salt, and nutmeg together. Combine the milk, ⅓ cup melted butter or oil, vanilla, and egg; then add to dry ingredients. Stir just until moistened. Do not beat. Spoon into greased muffin pans and bake at 400° for 20 minutes. Remove at once and dip each in the melted butter and roll in the sugar-cinnamon mixture.

Ahead of time: These can be done the day before and they freeze too, though they are at their very best right after they have been baked. If done the day before, keep in the refrigerator and reheat before serving. If frozen, defrost, then reheat in the oven.

Mincemeat Muffins

[makes 12]

¼ cup sugar	¾ cup milk
2 cups *Homemade Biscuit Mix, Handy Dandy No. 14, p. 12*	¼ cup salad oil
	1 egg
	¾ cup mincemeat

Add the sugar to the *Homemade Biscuit Mix* and place in a bowl. Beat together the milk, oil, and egg and stir in the mincemeat. Add this to the flour mixture and stir only until combined. Do not beat. Fill greased muffin tins about three-fourths full. Bake at 425° for about 20 minutes.

Ahead of time: These can be baked the day before and they can be frozen. They should be reheated and served hot.

Blueberry Muffins Simplified

[makes 12]

½ cup sugar
1½ cups *Self-Rising Flour,*
    Handy Dandy No. 13,
    p. 11 (do not sift)
¼ cup soft butter

1 egg, broken into a
    measuring cup, milk
    added to make 1 cup,
    and mixed with a fork
1 cup fresh blueberries

Combine the sugar and *Self-Rising Flour.* Cut in the butter, then add the egg-milk mixture. Stir, but do not beat. Fold in the blueberries. Fill greased muffin tins about two-thirds full. Bake at 400° for 20 to 25 minutes.

Ahead of time: These can be baked the day before and they freeze well too. Reheat before serving.

A Super-Easy and Quick Coffee Cake

1¾ cups flour (not sifted)
¾ cup sugar
½ teaspoon salt
2 teaspoons baking powder

1 egg, plus enough milk to
    measure 1 cup
1 teaspoon vanilla
½ cup melted butter or oil

for the topping
½ cup brown sugar (pack to
    measure)

3 to 5 teaspoons cinnamon
3 tablespoons butter

Place the dry ingredients in a bowl and mix thoroughly. Combine the milk, egg, vanilla, and ½ cup melted butter or oil, then pour over flour mixture and stir until combined; do not beat. Pour into a greased 9-inch-square pan. Sprinkle top with the brown sugar and cinnamon; then dot with the 3 tablespoons butter. Bake at 350° for about 30 to 35 minutes. Serve hot or warm.

Ahead of time: This can be done in the morning or the day before or can be frozen. Reheat covered with foil before serving.

Tip: Even easier—if you have some *Self-Rising Flour, Handy Dandy No. 13,* p.11, on hand, use 1¾ cups of it in place of the flour, salt, and baking powder listed in the ingredients.

Nifty Waffles

2 cups *Homemade Biscuit Mix, Handy Dandy No. 14,* p. 12 (do not sift)
2 eggs
1¼ cups milk (or a little more)
4 tablespoons melted butter (or oil)

Combine all ingredients and stir well. Bake in a waffle iron.

Ahead of time: The batter can be made the day before. Keep covered and refrigerated until time to cook the waffles. If the batter seems too thick, add a bit more milk.

German Pancake for Four

3 extra-large eggs
¼ teaspoon salt
½ cup flour
½ cup milk
2 tablespoons soft butter
powdered sugar
lemon juice or melted butter

Beat the eggs until light; add the salt and flour and then the milk, beating all the time. Spread a 10-inch cold skillet with the soft butter. Pour in the batter and bake in a 475° oven for 20 to 25 minutes, gradually reducing heat to about 350°. The pancake should puff up at the sides and be crisp and brown. Serve with powdered sugar and a choice of lemon juice or melted butter.

Ahead of time: The batter can be mixed several hours ahead of baking. Keep at room temperature.

≡*Easiest*

Thin, Thin Parmesan Melba Toasts

extra-thin sliced white bread   grated parmesan cheese
melted butter

Place bread on a baking pan (cookie pans are good). Cut in any desired sizes or shapes. Brush with melted butter and sprinkle with grated cheese. Bake in a 225° oven until dry, brown, and crisp.

Ahead of time: These can be made in the morning or the day before and they can be frozen. Reheat gently before serving.

Tip: These can be used in various ways: as an appetizer served either hot or at room temperature or with soups and salads. An extraordinarily delicious use for slightly stale bread. These are equally good made with thinly sliced rye or whole-wheat.

Something Different for Biscuits

[serves about 6]

1 cup Rice Krispies, crushed
2 tablespoons caraway
   seeds
½ teaspoon salt

1 package commercially
   prepared biscuits (in
   circular tube)
1 egg, slightly beaten

Mix the Rice Krispies, caraway seeds, and salt together. Dip each biscuit in beaten egg, then roll in the mixture and place on a greased baking sheet. Bake at 425° for 12 to 15 minutes. Serve very hot with plenty of butter.

Ahead of time: These can be readied in the morning; keep refrigerated until shortly before baking.

Cornbread in a Hurry

1 cup cornmeal	2 tablespoons sugar
1 cup flour (scant; not	1 egg
necessary to sift)	1 cup milk
3 teaspoons baking powder	⅓ cup salad oil
1 teaspoon salt	

Mix the dry ingredients together. Combine the egg, milk, and oil and add to the dry mixture, stirring only until blended. Bake in a greased 9-inch-square pan (or in greased muffin tins) at 400° for 20 to 25 minutes.

Ahead of time: Best baked and eaten fresh; however, this is really very good reheated the next day.

Pita Bread Sesame-Seeded

pita breads
soft butter
sesame seeds

Cut pita breads in quarters or sixths or eighths. Split them open and separate into pieces. Spread the rough sides with soft butter and sprinkle heavily with sesame seeds. Bake in the upper level of a 425° oven for about 10 minutes, or until toasted and crisp. Serve hot or at room temperature.

Ahead of time: These can be done several days ahead (or in the morning); store in tightly covered tins or in plastic bags, tightly closed. They freeze well too; defrost, then reheat to serve.

Tip: These are splendid to eat all by themselves, as a crunch appetizer with cocktails; they are good too with first courses and with salads.

Parmesan French Toast

sour-dough bread   grated parmesan cheese
soft butter

Generously butter slices of sour-dough bread. Sprinkle thickly
with parmesan. Bake in the upper part of a 400° oven until crisp
and browned (about 15 to 20 minutes).

Ahead of time: This can be readied in the morning; keep covered at room temperature until time to bake.

A Foolproof Yorkshire Pudding

[serves 4 to 6]

1 cup sifted flour   ½ cup water
¾ teaspoon salt   2 eggs, slightly beaten
½ cup milk (room   (room temperature)
   temperature)   1 teaspoon salad oil

Mix the flour and salt, add the milk, water, eggs, and oil, and
stir until smooth. (Let stand ½ hour to several hours.) Grease a
dish (or pour dripping from a roast) into a pan about 9 by 12
inches and pour in the batter. Place in a *cold oven* (yes, a cold
oven) and immediately turn temperature to 400°. Bake about 40
to 45 minutes. Serve hot with roast beef.

Ahead of time: The batter can be prepared in the morning for
evening serving. Cover and leave it at room temperature; if it
thickens slightly, add 1 or 2 tablespoons of milk or water and stir
well.

Champagne Muffins

[makes about 8 muffins]

1½ cups *Homemade Biscuit Mix, Handy Dandy No. 14,* p. 12

¼ cup sugar
¾ cup champagne
sweet butter

Mix the *Biscuit Mix* and sugar together. Add the champagne and stir, but only until ingredients are moistened; do not beat. Spoon into well-greased muffin tins. Bake at 425° for about 20 to 25 minutes. Serve very hot with plenty of chilled sweet butter.

Ahead of time: Although these reheat quite nicely, they are best eaten as soon as they have been baked. But why not use that ahead-of-time to make *Handy Dandy No. 14.*

Tip: If you can't spare the time (or space) to make your own biscuit mix, a commercial variety does just fine.

So-Simple Scones

[makes 8 wedges]

¼ cup soft butter
1 cup *Self-Rising Flour, Handy Dandy, No. 13,* p. 11

1 egg
3 tablespoons milk
granulated sugar

Cut the butter into the *Self-Rising Flour*. Combine the egg and milk and add; stir only until combined. Knead gently for a few seconds on a floured surface; then pat into a ½-inch-thick circle and sprinkle with sugar. Cut in 8 wedges. Place in a greased baking pan and bake at 425° for about 12 to 15 minutes. Serve hot with butter and jam.

Ahead of time: These can be prepared in the morning and kept refrigerated until time to bake. Add a few more minutes to the baking time if they are cold.

11/CAKES, COOKIES, AND CONFECTIONS

Exotic but Easy Macadamia and Pineapple Cakes

[makes 8 small or about 4 large cakes]

10 ounces salted macadamia nuts, cut in quarters or coarsely chopped	2 cups sugar
	7 extra-large eggs (or 8 regular size)
1 pound candied pineapple, diced (about 3 cups)	2 teaspoons vanilla
3½ cups sifted flour	1 teaspoon baking powder
1 pound butter	½ teaspoon cream of tartar

Combine the nuts and pineapple and mix with 2 cups of the flour. Cream the butter and sugar until fluffy, then beat in the eggs and vanilla. Sift the remaining flour with the baking powder and cream of tartar, and add. Now stir in the nut-pineapple-flour mixture and mix all until well combined. Spoon into about 8 small greased and floured loaf pans (or larger ones if you prefer). Bake at 325° for 30 minutes, then reduce oven to 300° and bake about another 45 minutes to 1 hour (a little longer if pans are large). Remove from oven and from the pans. Cool on racks. Wrap in plastic, then in foil.

Ahead of time: These can be kept refrigerated for a month; they can be frozen for six months. Serve at room temperature.

A Six-Layer Chocolate Dream

[serves about 16]

1 pound dark sweet chocolate	3 (9-inch) chocolate cake layers (use either chocolate cake recipe, p. 245)
1⅓ cups heavy cream	

Combine the chocolate and the whipping cream in the top of a double boiler and stir until well mixed and chocolate melted. Cool at room temperature. Cut each cake layer in half (thus making six). Place a layer on a plate and cover generously with the chocolate icing. Continue with other layers; finally cover top and sides with icing. Let the cake sit to dry a little (about 1 hour), then cover with plastic wrap until time to serve.

Ahead of time: This can be made 1 to 3 days before using. Keep covered and refrigerated, but allow about 3 hours out of refrigerator before serving. It freezes well too; be sure it is well defrosted and at room temperature before serving.

Chocolate Date and Walnut Cake with a Cinnamon Topping

[serves about 8]

3 ounces semisweet
   chocolate
1 ounce unsweetened
   chocolate
1¼ cups chopped dates
   (about ½ pound)
1 cup chopped walnuts,
   lightly toasted
4 tablespoons flour

¾ cup sugar (scant)
1 teaspoon baking powder
¼ teaspoon salt
2 eggs
2 tablespoons sugar
½ teaspoon cinnamon (or a
   little more)
whipped cream (optional)

Melt both kinds of chocolate over hot water. Cool. Combine the dates, nuts, and 2 tablespoons of the flour and toss. Combine the other 2 tablespoons flour with the ¾ cup sugar, the baking powder, and the salt. Beat the eggs until fluffy, then beat in the sugar-flour mixture; stir in the chocolate and then add the date-nut mixture. Pour into a well-greased and floured 9-inch round cake pan. Bake at 300° for 30 to 35 minutes, then at 250° for about 10 minutes. Remove from oven and cool on a rack about 5 minutes, then remove from pan and cover top with the 2 tablespoons sugar mixed with the cinnamon. Serve warm or at room temperature, with or without whipped cream.

Ahead of time: This can be baked the day before and it can be frozen; before serving I recommend reheating it (wrapped in foil) for a brief time in a 325° oven.

Mary Cullins' Molasses Cake

[serves 12 to 16]

1 cup butter
1 cup sugar
3 eggs
1 teaspoon baking soda
1 cup molasses
3 cups sifted flour
1 teaspoon ginger

¼ teaspoon nutmeg
¼ teaspoon ground cloves
¾ teaspoon salt
1 cup milk
½ cup chopped nuts
1 cup raisins

for the topping
1 cup powdered sugar
(pack to measure)

juice of 2 lemons

Make sure all ingredients are at room temperature. Cream the butter and sugar, then beat in the eggs. Add the soda to the molasses. Sift the dry ingredients together, then add alternately with the molasses and milk. Stir in the nuts and raisins. Bake in a greased and floured large pan (9 by 13 inches) at 350° for 45 to 50 minutes. Remove from oven. Combine the powdered sugar and lemon juice and spoon on top of cake while it is still warm.

Ahead of time: This can be made the day before. Cover well and refrigerate but bring to room temperature before serving.

Al Dragotto's Sister's Fruit Bars

[makes 48 or more]

2½ cups flour	2 eggs
1 cup sugar	grated rind of 1 orange
1 teaspoon baking soda	¼ cup orange juice
½ teaspoon salt	1 cup raisins
½ teaspoon nutmeg	½ cup chopped nuts
½ teaspoon cinnamon	1 cup chopped dates
½ cup soft butter (or shortening)	

for the icing

3 tablespoons milk	sifted powdered sugar
1 teaspoon vanilla	

Combine the dry ingredients and mix together (or sift together). Blend in the butter or shortening. Add the eggs, orange rind, and orange juice and mix well. Stir in the raisins, nuts, and dates. Divide into 6 longish rolls and place on 2 greased cookie sheets. Bake at 350° for about 18 to 20 minutes. Remove from oven and let cool. Make the icing by heating milk, then adding vanilla and enough powdered sugar to achieve the desired consistency. When the rolls are cold, frost with the icing and cut in diagonal bars.

Ahead of time: These can be baked several days ahead, frosted, cut in bars, and stored in airtight tins. They can be frozen, but freeze without frosting and cutting them. Frost before serving, then cut and serve.

Bathshebas

[makes 36 to 48]

1 pound powdered sugar	additional sieved
½ cup soft butter	powdered sugar
⅓ cup bourbon whiskey	
¾ cup pecans, toasted, then chopped	

for dipping

about ⅙ bar of paraffin (½ ounce)

11 ounces semisweet chocolate

1 ounce unsweetened chocolate

Cream the 1 pound powdered sugar with the butter (if possible, use an electric beater). Gradually beat in the bourbon. Stir in the pecans and chill for several hours. Roll the mixture into small balls (use the extra sieved powdered sugar on your hands while you make the balls). Place on waxed-paper-lined trays. Chill thoroughly. Melt the paraffin in the top of a double boiler. Add all the chocolate and stir to melt, but keep water only hot, *not* bubbling. Dip the chilled *Bathshebas* in the chocolate and place them on waxed paper. Chill again. Pack them in foil-lined, airtight tins and keep refrigerated.

Ahead of time: These keep very well for 1 or 2 weeks in the refrigerator.

Tip: I like to serve these directly from the refrigerator.

Magic Mix Chez Mellinkoff

2 cups pecans
1⅓ cups blanched almonds
8 cups popped popcorn
(unsalted and
unbuttered)

1⅓ cups sugar
1 cup butter
½ cup white Karo syrup
1 teaspoon vanilla

Toast the nuts in a 325° oven (about 15 minutes); do not let them burn. Mix them with the popcorn and spread in a large buttered baking pan. Bring the sugar, butter, and syrup to a boil and cook over moderate heat, stirring constantly, until it boils. Then continue cooking and occasionally stirring until it is a light caramel (about 250° F on candy thermometer). Remove from heat and add the vanilla. Pour over the popcorn-nut mixture and stir well. Place in a 350° oven and bake for about 30 minutes, or until popcorn and nuts are glazed to a warm rich brown. Remove from oven and turn out onto lightly buttered foil. Cool completely, then store in airtight tins or jars.

Ahead of time: This will keep for weeks in airtight containers.

Noah's Ark Almond-Kirsch Cake

[serves 8 to 10]

⅔ cup butter
¾ cup sugar
3 eggs
½ cup blanched almonds,
    ground

½ cup sifted flour
¼ teaspoon salt
½ teaspoon baking powder
¼ cup kirsch

Cream the butter and sugar. Add the eggs and beat, then stir in the almonds. Sift the flour, salt, and baking powder together and add to the batter along with the kirsch. Bake at 350° in a greased and floured 8-inch spring-form pan (or layer-cake pan) for 30 to 35 minutes. Remove and cool.

Ahead of time: This can be baked the day before; it also freezes. Serve at room temperature.

Tip: This cake is lovely just as it is; however, it can be frosted with a thin powdered-sugar frosting flavored with kirsch, or with sieved apricot jam.

Balanced Cake with Peaches

[serves 8 to 10]

1¼ sticks butter (5 ounces)
¾ cup sugar
3 large eggs
¼ teaspoon salt
1½ teaspoons vanilla

1½ teaspoons baking powder
1 cup plus 2 tablespoons
    flour (5 ounces)
1 (1-pound) can sliced
    peaches

Make sure all ingredients are at room temperature. Cream the butter and sugar together, then beat in the eggs one at a time. Add the salt and vanilla. Sift the baking powder and flour together, then gradually stir into the mixture. Do not overbeat. Spoon into a greased and floured 9-inch springform pan. Drain the peaches.

Lay peaches lightly on top of the batter—some will sink during the baking process so do not press them into batter. Bake in a 350° oven for about 1 hour or until cake is done. Remove and place pan on a rack. After 5 minutes, remove side of pan and finish cooling. Serve at room temperature.

Ahead of time: This is best when freshly baked, but it is still very good the next day.

Molasses Spicy Pound Cake

[serves 12 to 16]

1 cup butter	2 teaspoons cloves
1¾ cups sugar	2 teaspoons soda
6 extra-large eggs	½ teaspoon salt
1 cup dark molasses	3 cups sifted flour
3 teaspoons cinnamon	1 cup sour cream
1 teaspoon nutmeg	

Make sure all ingredients are at room temperature. Cream the butter and sugar, then beat in the eggs one at a time. Beat in the molasses. Sift the dry ingredients together, then add alternately with the sour cream. Pour into a greased and floured 10-inch tube pan. Bake at 350° for 10 minutes. Reduce heat to 325° and bake an additional 40 to 50 minutes. Remove pan from oven and cool 5 minutes; then turn cake out of pan and finish cooling on a rack.

Ahead of time: This can be baked 1 or 2 days ahead; keep well wrapped and refrigerated. It can also be frozen. In either case be sure to serve it at room temperature.

Pecan Balls

[makes 36 to 48]

1 cup butter
½ cup sugar
2 teaspoons vanilla
2 cups sifted flour

2 cups pecans, measured
    and then ground
powdered sugar

Cream the butter and sugar, then add the vanilla and flour. Stir in the ground pecans. Shape into small balls (about the size of a walnut). Bake at 300° for 25 to 35 minutes. Remove from oven and while warm roll balls in powdered sugar.

Ahead of time: These can be done a week or more ahead (or longer if frozen). Keep them refrigerated or frozen in airtight tins.

Tip: Especially delicious served directly from refrigerator or freezer.

Chocolate-Covered Graham Crackers

[makes about 24]

⅙ bar of paraffin (about ½
    ounce)
2 ounces (2 squares)
    unsweetened chocolate

10 ounces semisweet
    chocolate
graham crackers

Melt the paraffin in the top of a double boiler over low heat. Add all the chocolate and stir over barely simmering water until smooth. (Do not allow chocolate to get too warm.) Remove from heat but keep over warm water to maintain spreading consistency. Dip the crackers in the chocolate (use tongs) and place on waxed paper to dry—about 3 to 4 hours or longer. Store in airtight jars or tins (either at room temperature or in refrigerator).

Ahead of time: These will keep for weeks in airtight containers. They freeze well too.

Tip: If you prefer a sweeter coating, use all semisweet chocolate. For those who loved the old-fashioned chocolate-covered grahams these are worth doing, since only a pseudo-chocolate covering is commercially available now.

Stuffed Figs Fancy

1 pound dried figs (very best quality)

¾ cup candied orange peel, finely chopped

¼ teaspoon powdered cloves

1 cup toasted whole almonds

¾ cup powdered sugar, sieved

⅓ cup cocoa

Trim away the hard stems of the figs. Cut each fig open on one side. Combine the orange peel and cloves and use this and the almonds to stuff the figs. I use about 1 teaspoon of the clove-orange peel and 2 almonds for each fig. Press figs closed and place on a baking sheet. Bake at 350° for 10 to 15 minutes. While figs are baking, mix the powdered sugar and cocoa together. Remove figs from oven and immediately roll them in the powdered sugar–cocoa mixture. Let them cool, then pack between layers of waxed paper and store in airtight tins.

Ahead of time: These can be prepared 1 to 2 weeks ahead of time. I keep them refrigerated but bring them to room temperature 3 to 4 hours before serving.

Regina Neuman's Moist Chocolate Cake

[makes one 9- by 13-inch cake, or three 9-inch round layers]

3 cups sifted flour (13½ ounces)
2 cups sugar
¾ cup cocoa (sifted or sieved to remove lumps)
2 teaspoons soda
1 teaspoon salt
2 tablespoons vinegar
2 teaspoons vanilla
¾ cup salad oil
2⅔ cups cold water

Combine all dry ingredients and mix well. Make three holes in the mixture and pour the vinegar in one; the vanilla in the second; and the oil in the third. Pour the water over all and mix with a fork (or whisk) until smooth. Pour into a greased and floured pan or pans. Bake at 350°—50 minutes or so for one large cake; about 25 minutes for layers.

Ahead of time: This cake can be baked ahead and frozen; just defrost and bring to room temperature before serving.

Tip: This can be served with nothing more than a generous sprinkling of powdered sugar, or it can become elaborately rich with a dark chocolate icing.

A Basic Simple Chocolate Cake

[makes three 9-inch round layers]

3 squares unsweetened chocolate
½ cup butter
2 cups sifted cake flour (7 ounces)
½ teaspoon baking powder
1½ teaspoons baking soda
1 teaspoon salt (scant)
1 teaspoon cinnamon
2 cups sugar
1¼ cups milk
3 eggs
2 teaspoons vanilla

Melt the chocolate and butter together over lowest heat or in top of double boiler and set aside to cool somewhat. Combine the dry ingredients in a large bowl and mix thoroughly. Combine the milk, eggs, and vanilla in another bowl and mix thoroughly. Add the liquid mixture to the dry and mix only until barely combined; add the melted chocolate and butter and mix only until combined. Do not beat. Pour into 3 greased and floured 9-inch pans and bake at 350° for about 25 minutes.

Ahead of time: These can be baked and frozen. Serve at room temperature.

A Basic Simple Yellow Cake

[makes three 9-inch round layers]

3 cups sifted cake flour (10½ ounces)	1 cup milk
2 cups sugar	4 eggs
¾ teaspoon salt	1½ teaspoons vanilla
3 teaspoons baking powder	1 cup melted butter

Combine the dry ingredients in a large bowl and mix thoroughly. Combine the milk, eggs, vanilla, and butter in another bowl and mix thoroughly. Add the liquid ingredients to the dry and mix only until well combined. Do not beat. Pour into three greased and floured 9-inch pans and bake at 350° for about 25 minutes.

Ahead of time: These can be baked and frozen. Serve at room temperature.

Tip: This batter also makes excellent cupcakes.

Easier-Than-a-Mix Pineapple Cake

[serves 12 to 16]

2 cups flour (measure by
  spooning flour lightly
  into cup)
½ teaspoon salt
1 teaspoon baking soda
1½ cups sugar

⅓ cup brown sugar (pack to
  measure)
1 cup chopped walnuts
2 eggs
1 (1-pound, 4-ounce) can
  crushed pineapple (do
  not drain)

for the icing
½ cup butter
⅓ cup milk
⅔ cup sugar

1 cup shredded or flaked
  coconut

Combine the flour, salt, soda, sugars, and walnuts in a large bowl and mix thoroughly (use your hands). Combine the eggs with the undrained pineapple and add to the dry ingredients. Mix well, then pour into a lightly greased 9-by-13-inch pan. Bake at 350° for about 35 to 40 minutes. Make the icing by heating the butter, milk, and sugar until sugar has dissolved. When cake is done place on a cooling rack and while it is still warm pour the icing over it. Sprinkle the top with the coconut.

Ahead of time: This can be made a day ahead; and it does freeze. Be sure to serve at room temperature.

Rum Cake Best and Easiest

[serves about 8]

½ cup butter
1 cup sugar
1 cup light rum

1 (9-inch) layer yellow cake,
  bought or homemade;
  you can use *Basic Simple
  Yellow Cake*, p. 246

Combine the butter and sugar over low heat and stir until sugar has dissolved. Remove from heat and add the rum. Place the cake on a large plate and punch holes in it with a fork. Spoon the rum sauce onto the cake. It will gradually absorb all (or most of) the sauce. Serve at room temperature.

Ahead of time: This can be prepared several days ahead. Keep covered and refrigerated, but bring to room temperature before serving.

Tip: For a "lighter" cake, use only half the amount of rum sauce. This rum cake can be served with just a sprinkling of powdered sugar, or it can be topped with fresh or canned fruit, or with custard or whipped cream, or with ice cream to make it a "frozen" cake.

Pat Altman's Tosca Cake

[serves about 8]

½ cup sugar
2 tablespoons flour
½ cup butter
2 tablespoons milk
½ teaspoon vanilla
1 cup sliced blanched
    almonds

1 (9- or 10-inch) layer sponge cake or butter cake, bought or homemade; you can use *Basic Simple Yellow Cake,* p. 246

Mix the sugar and flour together in a saucepan. Add the butter, milk, vanilla, and almonds. Cook over low heat, stirring constantly, until butter has melted and sugar is dissolved. Place the cake layer on an ovenproof dish. Spread the almond glaze on the cake, leaving 1 inch around the edge uncovered. Place under broiler until glaze is golden brown. Watch that it doesn't burn. Remove from oven and serve warm or at room temperature.

Ahead of time: This can be done in the morning or the day before. To serve warm, reheat for a short time before serving. The same instructions apply if you freeze it.

Chocolate Cake, Pears, and Chocolate Glaze Paradise

[serves about 12]

12 ounces dark sweet
   chocolate
1 cup heavy cream
12 to 14 canned pear halves,
   well drained

2 (9-inch) round chocolate
   cake layers, bought or
   homemade (you can
   use the chocolate cakes
   on p. 245)

Combine the chocolate and cream over simmering water and stir (or whisk) until melted and combined. Remove and cool at room temperature. Place the pear halves rounded side up on both cake layers (6 or 7, depending on size of pears). When the glaze has thickened, spoon it over the pears and cake layers generously. Serve at room temperature or chilled.

Ahead of time: This can be completely assembled in the morning. Cover lightly with plastic wrap and leave at room temperature (or refrigerate). The glaze can be made days or weeks ahead and kept refrigerated (or in the freezer for months). Bring to spooning consistency by heating it gently. Homemade layer cakes can be frozen; defrost and bring to room temperature before using.

Deliciously Simple Cookies

1 cup butter
1 cup sugar
¼ cup milk

2 cups flour
¼ teaspoon salt
2 teaspoons vanilla

Cream the butter and sugar. Add the milk, then add the remaining ingredients. Combine and make the dough into 2 rolls. Chill, then slice and bake at 350° (10 to 15 minutes).

Ahead of time: These can be baked several days or a week ahead. Keep packed between layers of waxed paper in airtight tins. And they can be frozen either baked or unbaked. If unbaked, freeze as rolls, well wrapped. Defrost only enough to slice them for baking.

Butterscotch-Pecan Bars

½ cup butter
2 cups brown sugar
   (packed)
2 eggs
2 teaspoons vanilla

1 cup sifted flour
2 teaspoons baking powder
1½ cups chopped pecans
   (lightly toasted)

Melt the butter, then stir in the brown sugar and place in a large bowl. Beat in the eggs and vanilla, then sift the dry ingredients together and add. Stir in the pecans. Bake in a greased 9-by-13-inch pan at 350° for 25 to 30 minutes. Cool, then cut into bars.

Ahead of time: These can be prepared the day before; the bars freeze well too.

Chocolate-Chip Brownies

4 ounces (4 squares)
   unsweetened chocolate
1 cup butter
4 eggs
2 cups sugar

1 cup sifted flour
pinch of salt
2 teaspoons vanilla
2 cups chocolate chips

Melt the chocolate unsweetened with the butter over low heat, then cool. Beat the eggs and sugar until thick and light, then add the chocolate-butter mixture. Stir in the remaining ingredients. Pour into a greased 9-by-13-inch pan and bake at 350° for about 25 to 30 minutes. Remove and cool, then cut into squares.

Ahead of time: These can be baked the day before and they freeze well. Serve at room temperature, or cover with foil and re-heat very briefly, then serve warm.

Tip: This one is definitely for chocolate lovers; if preferred, walnuts can be substituted for the chocolate chips.

Date Caramel Bars

½ cup butter
2 cups brown sugar
  (packed)
2 eggs
2 teaspoons vanilla

1 cup sifted flour
2 teaspoons baking powder
½ teaspoon salt
2 cups chopped dates

Melt the butter, then combine with the brown sugar in a large bowl. Beat in the eggs, then add vanilla. Sift the dry ingredients together and add. Stir in the dates and spoon the batter into a greased and floured 9-by-13-inch pan. Bake at 350° for about 30 minutes. Cool and cut into bars.

Ahead of time: These can be baked a day or so ahead. Keep packed in an airtight container between layers of waxed paper. These freeze well too.

Chocolate Ganache Squares

1 pound dark sweet
  chocolate
1 cup heavy cream

1 tablespoon dark rum
toasted walnut halves

Melt the chocolate over barely simmering water. Heat the cream to hot (but not boiling) and beat into the chocolate. Beat in the rum. Set aside to cool, whipping or stirring occasionally. Spread the mixture in a buttered 8-inch-square pan. Chill, then when beginning to firm up, mark in squares and top each with a walnut half. When completely cold, cut and remove to an airtight tin. (Pack between layers of waxed paper.) Keep refrigerated.

Ahead of time: These can be prepared 1 to 2 weeks ahead. Keep refrigerated.

Peanut-Butter Chocolate Fudge

2 cups sugar
⅛ teaspoon salt
3 ounces (3 squares)
    unsweetened chocolate
¾ cup evaporated milk

1 teaspoon vanilla
1 tablespoon butter
6 ounces chunky-style
    peanut butter (a little
    more than ½ cup)

Combine sugar, salt, chocolate, and evaporated milk in a sauce-pan and cook over low to moderate heat, stirring, until mixture boils. Continue cooking on low heat for 5 minutes (it should bubble gently). Remove from heat and add the remaining ingredients. Beat for 4 minutes and pour into a well-buttered 8-inch-square pan.

Ahead of time: This can be made several days ahead and if covered well and refrigerated will keep excellently. It freezes too. In either case, be sure to bring it to room temperature before serving.

12/DESSERTS

A Rum Cake Amusement

[serves 8]

1 package frozen
  raspberries, defrosted
½ cup seedless raspberry
  jam
8 canned pear halves,
  drained and dried
1 layer of *Rum Cake Best and
  Easiest*, p. 247 (made
  with half the rum
  sauce)

1 cup *Whipped Cream
  Immobilized, Handy
  Dandy No. 18*, p. 15

Purée the raspberries, then strain to remove seeds. Combine the purée with the jam and cook 1 or 2 minutes. Cool, then chill. Place the pears (rounded side up) on the cake. Spoon a little of the chilled sauce on each pear; serve the rest separately at the table. Decorate the cake with the *Whipped Cream Immobilized*. Chill.

Ahead of time: The *Rum Cake* can be prepared several days ahead as directed in that recipe. The dessert can be completely assembled in the morning; cover and refrigerate until time to serve.

Coffee-Macaroon Fantasia

[serves 12]

36 almond macaroons
¾ cup dark Jamaican rum
2 quarts coffee ice cream

2 cups whipping cream
¼ cup sugar
1 tablespoon rum

Toast 12 of the macaroons in a 275° oven. Crumble them with a rolling pin. Place the 24 remaining macaroons on a large platter and punch the tops with a fork, then dribble the ¾ cup rum over them. Let them stand until well soaked. Arrange 12 dessert bowls with, first, a layer of ice cream, then a soaked macaroon (use a spatula to lift them); then a second layer of ice cream and another macaroon; then top with a third layer of ice cream. Place in freezer. Whip the cream with the sugar and 1 tablespoon rum. Just before serving, take out the dessert, spread whipped cream on top, and sprinkle with the toasted macaroon crumbs.

Ahead of time: These can be completely assembled 2 days before serving. Cover each with plastic wrap and leave in freezer until time to serve.

Rainbow Sherbet Kirsch Cake

[serves 12 to 16]

½ cup sugar
½ cup water
½ cup kirsch
1 large sponge cake (bought is fine)
¾ cup seedless raspberry jam

1 pint raspberry sherbet
1 pint pineapple sherbet
1 pint orange sherbet
2 cups whipping cream
⅓ cup sugar
3 tablespoons kirsch

Combine the ½ cup sugar with the water, then cook over low heat until sugar has dissolved. Remove from heat and add the ½ cup kirsch. Cut the cake into four layers. Place one layer on a serving dish and sprinkle with about one-fourth of the prepared syrup. Spread with one-third of the jam (one-fourth cup) and cover with the raspberry sherbet. Cover with a second cake layer and repeat, using the pineapple sherbet, then add a third cake layer and again repeat, using the orange sherbet. Top with the fourth cake layer and sprinkle with the remaining one-fourth of the syrup. Place in freezer until frozen. Whip the cream with the ⅓ cup sugar and flavor with the 3 tablespoons kirsch. Use this to frost the frozen cake, then return it to the freezer. Remove from freezer about 20 to 30 minutes before serving time; otherwise the cake will be too hard to cut.

Ahead of time: This can be made about 10 days ahead; cover and keep frozen until needed.

Tip: This makes an excellent and unusual birthday cake. Try serving it with a raspberry or strawberry sauce on the side.

A Virtuous Garden of Delights

[serves many or few]

miniature babas au rhum,
canned
tiny balls of vanilla ice
cream (made with a
melon-ball scoop)

fresh raspberries

for the chocolate sauce
8 ounces dark sweet
chocolate
1 cup heavy cream (or
more, depending on
thinness you want)

a little rum or brandy to
taste

for the raspberry purée
frozen raspberries
sugar to taste

framboise liqueur to taste

other fruits of the season
fresh strawberries
fresh pineapple, sliced
cantaloupe balls

watermelon balls
peaches, peeled and
quartered

To make the chocolate sauce: Combine the chocolate and cream
and cook over low heat, stirring often, until chocolate is melted.
Add the rum or brandy. Serve hot or cold. (This recipe can be
doubled or tripled.) To make the raspberry purée: Defrost berries. Purée them and then sieve to eliminate the seeds. Sweeten
and flavor to taste. Serve cold. To assemble: Arrange the "garden" either on several large platters or on a cart or side table.
Items should be arranged something like this:

1 miniature babas au rhum on a flat serving dish
2 tiny ice cream balls in a bowl
3 chocolate sauce in a bowl next to the ice cream
4 fresh raspberries in a bowl or on a dish
5 raspberry purée in a bowl next to the raspberries
6 other fruits arranged in separate "bouquets" on dishes or
platters

Either let guests help themselves, or better, serve each person a large plate with one miniature baba, one ice cream ball with chocolate sauce over it, a spoonful of raspberries with raspberry purée over them, and a sampling of the other fruits arranged in miniature "bouquets" on the plate.

Ahead of time: The chocolate sauce can be made days ahead; the raspberry purée can be made the day before. The ice cream balls can be made and kept covered in the freezer until you are ready to arrange the dessert.

Tip: Serve this on large dinner plates so that each of the virtuous delights can be separately visible.

Bananas Foster—My Style

[serves 6]

½ cup butter
1 cup dark brown sugar
   (pack to measure)
1 teaspoon cinnamon
4 large bananas, sliced
   lengthwise, then sliced
   in half again crosswise

3 tablespoons dark Jamaican
   rum
3 tablespoons 151 proof
   rum (see *The Magic
   Torch, Handy Dandy No.
   17,* p. 14
6 portions vanilla ice cream

Melt the butter in a chafing dish, add the sugar and cinnamon, and cook until bubbling. Add the bananas and cook very briefly, turning once or twice. Add the Jamaican rum and stir. Add the 151 proof rum and flame. Serve over vanilla ice cream.

Ahead of time: Arrange all needed ingredients (except the ice cream) on a tray along with the chafing dish. Put the ice cream in dessert bowls or dishes in the freezer.

Tip: Don't worry that the sauce takes a little time to bubble. Your guests will enjoy the spectacle and the wait; all you need do is share their patience.

Empyrean Strawberries

large, ripe strawberries
(preferably with long
stems)
1 egg white

1 tablespoon water
powdered sugar
red food coloring

Clean the strawberries but do not remove the stems. Do this several hours ahead and leave the berries at room temperature on paper towels; they need to be completely dry. Beat the egg white and water together slightly, then gradually add powdered sugar until mixture is of a thin spreading consistency. Add a very tiny touch of red coloring to make the glaze a very light pink. (Dip a toothpick in the color to avoid getting too much.) Barely warm this mixture, then, holding the strawberries by the stem ends, dip them into the pink glaze but do not wholly cover them. Place on a cake rack, with the stem end down, and let dry. Leave at room temperature, uncovered.

Ahead of time: The glaze can be made in the morning or the day before, but the strawberries should be dipped not more than 2 to 3 hours before they are to be eaten. If they stand too long the glaze will disintegrate.

Aphrodite's Apples with Almonds

[serves about 6]

6 cups peeled sliced green
apples
1¼ cups brown sugar (pack
to measure)
⅓ cup butter
⅛ teaspoon salt

½ teaspoon cinnamon
1 cup flour
1 cup toasted slivered
almonds
chilled heavy cream

Place the apples in an attractive shallow casserole. Cover with half the sugar. Combine the remaining sugar, the butter, salt, cinnamon, and flour, and mix thoroughly either with your hands or with a fork or pastry blender. Pat the mixture on top of the apples, covering them completely. Bake for 35 minutes at

350°. Now, cover the top with the almonds, pressing down well. Return to oven and bake an additional 25 minutes. Serve hot or warm and pass the cream in a pitcher.

Ahead of time: This can be baked the day before and reheated; it freezes well too. Excellent also served chilled.

Amiable Apple Slices
[serves 8 to 10]

> 2 cups *Homemade Biscuit Mix, Handy Dandy No. 14,* p. 12
> 2 tablespoons sugar
>
> 2 eggs
> 1 cup milk
> 6 apples, peeled, cored, and sliced

for the topping
> ½ cup butter
> 1 cup powdered sugar
>
> 1 teaspoon vanilla

Combine the *Biscuit Mix* with the sugar. Mix the eggs and milk together, then add and stir but do not beat. Spoon into a greased and floured 9-by-13-inch pan. Cover with the sliced apples and bake at 350° for 40 to 50 minutes. While the cake is baking, make the topping. Cream the butter and powdered sugar together, then add vanilla. While the cake is still hot, spread topping over it, then cool slightly.

Ahead of time: This can be made ahead of time, but I prefer it right after it has been baked. If made in advance, reheat briefly before serving.

Tip: Not necessary but extra good—serve with vanilla ice cream.

Praline Ice Cream

[serves 12 to 14]

1 cup sugar
1 scant cup finely diced
    almonds

2 quarts vanilla ice cream

Melt the sugar in a heavy skillet over moderate heat until cara-melized, stirring occasionally so it caramelizes evenly. Add the almonds and stir until combined. Be careful not to burn the sug-ar. Pour this praline into a shallow, lightly greased metal pan and set aside until cold. Break or pound the praline into pea-sized pieces. (Cover praline with plastic wrap, or place in a plas-tic bag while you pound; this stops it from flying all over the kitchen.) Put the ice cream in a large bowl and let soften only slightly, then work in the prepared praline, stirring only as much as is necessary to combine. Refreeze.

Ahead of time: This obviously must be done ahead of time. The praline can be done weeks ahead and stored in glass jars in the refrigerator. The praline ice cream should keep several weeks or longer in the freezer.

Chocolate Cups with Vanilla Ice Cream and Brandied Cherries

[serves 8]

½ pound dark sweet
    chocolate
3 tablespoons butter
    vanilla ice cream (about 1
    pint)

brandied cherries (use
    *Nonesuch Cherries, Handy
    Dandy No. 19,* p. 16, or
    *Brandied Bing Cherries,
    Handy Dandy No. 20,*
    p. 16

Melt chocolate with the butter slowly over warm water. Remove from heat and stir until blended. Cool briefly. Place 8 cupcake papers inside muffin pans—the regular size. Using a teaspoon, swirl the chocolate around the sides and bottoms of the cups, covering them with a thin layer of chocolate. Chill, then check to see if all the paper has been covered; if not, repair any thin spots or tiny holes with thin dabs of melted chocolate. Chill again. Later peel off the paper cups and return the chocolate cups to refrigerator (or freezer) until time to use. Fill the cups with ice cream, then, using a small spoon (or melon-ball scoop), press down in center of ice cream to create an indentation. Fill each hollow with 2 brandied cherries and a little syrup.

Ahead of time: The chocolate cups can be made several days ahead. Keep covered and refrigerated. Or, they can be frozen, either unfilled or filled with the ice cream but not with the cherries. If you plan to freeze them for only a few days, it is not necessary to cover them; for long storage they must be well wrapped or stored in airtight cookie tins in the freezer.

Tip: You can dream up dozens of marvelous variations for filling these delectable chocolate cups; just let your imagination run wild.

Ice Cream with Burnt Caramel, Bananas, and Chopped Almonds

[serves 8]

1 quart vanilla ice cream	½ to 1 cup chopped toasted
3 bananas, sliced	almonds

for the burnt caramel sauce

2 cups sugar	1¼ cups boiling water

Make the sauce: Melt the sugar to a caramel over moderate heat, stirring often. Turn heat to lowest possible point, then add the boiling water. Watch out—it may sputter. Stir over low heat until water and sugar have completely combined. Cool to room temperature, then pour into a jar with a tight-fitting cover and refrigerate. To serve, scoop ice cream into individual dishes. Surround each serving with sliced bananas. Spoon some of the burnt caramel sauce (cold or at room temperature) on each, then top with toasted almonds.

Ahead of time: The caramel sauce will keep for weeks in the refrigerator.

Easier

Ravishing Peaches

[serves 12]

12 servings vanilla ice cream

assembled on tray or trays

1 cup butter, sliced	12 peach halves (fresh or
2⅔ cups brown sugar (pack	canned)
to measure)	½ cup cognac or brandy
⅔ cup heavy cream	2 tablespoons from *The*
2 to 3 teaspoons ground	*Magic Torch, Handy*
nutmeg (use a generous	*Dandy No. 17*, p. 14
amount)	

Have the ice cream ready in large individual bowls in the freezer. Melt the butter in the blazer of a large chafing dish. Let it sizzle, then add the sugar, cream, and nutmeg. Stir and cook; syrup must ultimately thicken a little. Add the peaches and continue to cook, spooning sauce over the peaches. Don't try to hurry this dessert; it takes time but your guests will enjoy watching the process. After the peaches have been well heated and sauce is bubbling, add the cognac, and finally, add *Magic Torch*, ignite the sauce, and spoon it flaming over the peaches. Serve half a peach on each portion of ice cream with plenty of sauce.

Ahead of time: All the ingredients can be assembled in bowls on trays in the morning.

Tip: This may be too many for some households to serve; don't hesitate to cut the recipe in half or less. If you lack a large freezer, ask one of your guests to dish up the ice cream while you prepare the *Ravishing Peaches*.

Flaming Tropical Cheer

[serves 8 to 10]

3 bananas, sliced ½-inch thick

1½ cups grated coconut (fresh or canned)

1 cup diced pineapple (fresh, canned, or frozen)

2 cups *Apricot Preserves, Handy Dandy No. 21,* p. 17

½ cup coarsely chopped walnuts, toasted

1 quart vanilla ice cream

⅓ cup *The Magic Torch, Handy Dandy No. 17,* p. 14

Arrange the bananas, coconut, and pineapple in bowls on a tray. Place the *Apricot Preserves* in a chafing dish, add the walnuts, and heat. Put the servings of ice cream in large dessert dishes. Add bananas, coconut, and pineapple to each portion. Add *Magic Torch* to the preserves and ignite. As soon as the flames burn out, spoon some sauce on each serving.

Ahead of time: If you have space in your freezer, put the ice cream in it in dessert glasses or bowls ahead of time. The *Apricot Preserves* can be prepared months in advance.

Chocolate Walnut Charm on Vanilla Ice Cream

[serves 6 to 8]

2 cups chopped walnuts

½ cup butter

12 ounces dark sweet chocolate

⅓ cup hot coffee (more or less)

vanilla ice cream

Sauté the walnuts gently in the butter over moderate heat until lightly browned. Add the chocolate and stir over lowest heat until barely melted. Add the coffee and stir. Serve hot over ice cream.

Ahead of time: The chocolate walnut sauce can be made several days ahead, then reheated. The ice cream can be (and if possible should be) spooned into dessert dishes or glasses ahead of time and kept in the freezer.

Tip: Add the hot coffee to the sauce gradually. The sauce should be of medium thickness—not too thick, as it will thicken on the cold ice cream, or too thin, or it will lose its quality.

A Blissful Bread Pudding with Caramel

[serves 4 to 6]

4 slices firm white bread	2 cups milk
2 tablespoons soft butter	3 eggs
1 cup brown sugar (pack to measure)	1 teaspoon vanilla
½ cup raisins	¼ teaspoon salt

Butter the bread slices, then cut them in cubes. Place the brown sugar in a 1½-quart casserole and pat down firmly. Sprinkle the bread cubes on top, then put the raisins over the bread. Heat the milk slightly. Beat the eggs with the vanilla, salt, and milk, then pour over bread and raisins gently so as not to disturb the sugar, or at least to disturb it as little as possible. Place the casserole in a pan of hot water and bake in a 325° oven until the custard is firm—about 1 hour. Serve hot or cold.

Ahead of time: This can be made the day before; in that case serve it cold.

Tip: You might like to serve this with a pitcher of heavy cream to be passed among your guests.

Pineapple Frozen Drunkenness

[serves about 6]

1½ cups puréed fresh
    pineapple (or grated or
    ground)
1½ cups chablis (or other dry
    white wine)

1½ cups sugar
1 tablespoon dark Jamaican
    rum
⅓ cup dry Bacardi rum
    (medium or light)

Combine all the ingredients and stir occasionally until the sugar
has dissolved. Freeze (it will never become solid); stir and freeze
again. Cover and keep in freezer until ready to use.

Ahead of time: This can be made several weeks ahead and kept
covered in the freezer.

Tip: Serve this marvelous concoction in wine glasses. If space
permits, spoon it into the glasses the morning of your dinner
and keep in the freezer until time to serve.

"Champagne" Sherbet in the Manner of the Capital Hotel

[serves about 6]

¾ cup water
1½ cups sugar
¼ cup lemon juice
1¾ cups chablis (or other dry
    white wine)

¼ cup fine champagne
    cognac (in theory only;
    use any good California
    or French brandy)

Combine the water and sugar in a saucepan and bring to a boil
over moderate heat, stirring to dissolve sugar. Remove and cool.
Add the remaining ingredients and pour the mixture into a large
flat pan (enamel or glass or stainless steel) and freeze until somewhat firm. Stir and again freeze until somewhat firm. Stir again,
then spoon the sherbet into goblets and leave in freezer until
ready to serve.

Ahead of time: This can be made several weeks ahead of time and left covered tightly in a large bowl in the freezer. The day you plan to serve it, stir it well and then place it in goblets.

Tip: Do not worry because this doesn't freeze really hard; it shouldn't since it has such a high percentage of alcohol.

A Winsome Strawberry Ice

[serves 6 to 8]

about 1 quart fresh strawberries, puréed (2 cups purée)	¾ cup sugar (about) ¼ cup water ¼ cup lemon juice

Combine all ingredients and stir until the sugar has dissolved. Freeze until mushy, then beat well and freeze again until almost firm. Beat again, then place in a covered container in the freezer until ready to serve.

Ahead of time: This should keep for several weeks in the freezer.

Tip: This is easier to serve if it is spooned into dessert dishes or glasses the morning of the party, then frozen until about 5 to 10 minutes before serving. It should be taken out of the freezer a little bit ahead of serving time so it won't be rock-hard.

Gloria Nimmer's Rhubarb Delight

[serves 8]

2 cups water
1 scant cup sugar
1¼ pounds rhubarb, cleaned
    and cut into 1½-inch
    diagonal pieces

1 box fresh strawberries,
    cleaned and hulled
    squeeze of lemon
¼ cup kirsch

Bring the water to a boil; stir in the sugar. Add the rhubarb all at once and bring to a boil again. Remove from heat immediately and add the strawberries, leave the pot covered for 1 or 2 minutes so that the strawberries soften but do not become soggy. Then remove the cover and cool the whole pot by immersing in cold water; this will prevent further cooking. Add a squeeze of lemon and the kirsch. Cover and chill until time to serve.

Ahead of time: This can be done the day before or in the morning.

Tip: Gloria suggests this as a refreshing dessert in warm weather or as dessert after any rich meal. She serves it in a crystal glass bowl garnished with mint leaves.

Chocolate-Orange Flaming Enchantment

[serves 4 to 6]

Dark, Rich, Hot Fudge
Sauce (recipe follows)
⅓ cup chopped toasted
almonds
1 generous tablespoon
grated orange rind

2 ounces *Magic Torch, Handy*
Dandy No. 17, p. 14
4 or 6 servings vanilla ice
cream

Dark, Rich, Hot Fudge Sauce

2 ounces (2 squares)
unsweetened chocolate
2 tablespoons butter
⅓ cup boiling water

1 cup sugar
2 tablespoons light corn
syrup
1 teaspoon vanilla

Make the fudge sauce. Melt the chocolate and 1 tablespoon of the butter over low heat and stir. Add the boiling water and blend, then stir in the sugar and syrup. Cook over low heat for 3 to 4 minutes. Remove, then add the remaining 1 tablespoon butter and the vanilla. Place it in the blazer of a chafing dish and add the toasted almonds and orange rind. Bring to the table; heat and stir before your guests. When hot and bubbling add *Magic Torch* and flame. Spoon the sauce over the ice cream and serve.

Ahead of time: The hot fudge sauce can be prepared several days ahead; keep refrigerated and reheat (stirring) before using. If you have room in the freezer it is best to dish up the ice cream beforehand.

Patricia Milner's Perfect Syllabub

[serves 8 to 10]

juice and grated rind of
1½ lemons
1 cup plus 2 tablespoons
sugar

6 tablespoons medium-dry
sherry
2 cups heavy whipping
cream

Combine the lemon juice and rind with the sugar and sherry. Stir until sugar has dissolved. Chill. Combine with the cream and whip until moderately stiff. Spoon over individual servings of fruit, or serve alone in elegant wine glasses.

Ahead of time: The lemon-sugar-sherry mixture should be done at least several hours ahead, or the day before, and kept refrigerated. I have successfully completed the syllabub in the morning, keeping it refrigerated until serving time.

Tip: The Milners serve this marvelous syllabub over real home-grown raspberries; since most of us are not that fortunate, choose whatever fresh fruit you like best. In the winter it can be served over sliced bananas or drained canned apricots, or, as suggested in the recipe, by itself. Accompany it with something like *Deliciously Simple Cookies*, p. 249.

A Captivating Avocado Dessert—from Kassim

[serves 4 to 6]

3 small or 2 large ripe
avocados
2 tablespoons cognac
2 tablespoons sherry

2 tablespoons Golden Syrup
(English, available in
specialty food stores)
1 cup heavy cream

Mash the avocados in a bowl with a fork. Gradually whip in the remaining ingredients—if possible with an electric beater (otherwise with a hand rotary beater or whisk). Spoon into tall, narrow glasses or into dessert glasses. Cover each tightly with plastic wrap and chill until time to serve.

Ahead of time: This can be prepared in the morning.

Very Lemon Ice Cream

[serves 6 to 8]

grated rind of 3 lemons
½ cup lemon juice

1 cup sugar
2 cups heavy cream

Combine all ingredients and stir occasionally until the sugar has dissolved. Pour into attractive dishes or glasses or cups and freeze until time to serve.

Ahead of time: This can be done a week ahead. Cover each with plastic wrap or with foil.

Lemon Sherbet, Gingered

fine-quality lemon sherbet
chopped candied ginger
(about 1 or 2 teaspoons per serving)

Place generous portions of the sherbet in dessert dishes or glasses. Top each with chopped candied ginger.

Ahead of time: If you have a freezer with plenty of space, these can be arranged with the ginger the day before or in the morning and kept frozen until time to serve.

Tip: Also nice topped with fresh strawberries or raspberries.

Rum-Raisin Ice Cream

[serves 6 to 8]

½ cup dark Jamaican rum   1 quart vanilla ice cream
1 cup dark raisins

Heat the rum slightly; don't let it boil. Pour it over the raisins and let them soak for several hours, then chill. Soften the ice cream only enough to beat in the rum-soaked raisins, then quickly refreeze.

Ahead of time: This can be prepared several weeks ahead. Keep well covered in the freezer.

Tip: This is especially attractive served in small goblets.

Chocolate-Coffee-Rum-Toffee Ice Cream Dazzler

chocolate ice cream
English toffee (or Heath candy bars), chopped (place in a plastic bag, then pound away)

ladyfingers, cut in half
dark Jamaican rum
coffee ice cream

Use tall glasses if possible, for maximum delight. Place a small-ish scoop of chocolate ice cream in the bottom of each glass. Sprinkle with a generous teaspoon of the chopped toffee. Place half a ladyfinger on top and sprinkle it with 1 or 2 teaspoons rum. Add a scoop of coffee ice cream and top off all with more of the toffee.

Ahead of time: Place the filled glasses in freezer up to a day before—then serve icy and frosty directly from freezer. It isn't necessary to cover or wrap these unless you plan to store them longer than 24 hours.

A Hush-Hush Ginger Mousse

[serves 8]

1 cup milk
18 large marshmallows
1 cup coarsely chopped preserved ginger

1 cup heavy cream, whipped
½ cup toasted almonds (or more if you like)

Heat the milk over low heat, add the marshmallows, and stir until they are melted. Cool, then chill briefly. Fold in the chopped ginger and whipped cream. Spoon into tiny crocks or dessert dishes. Cover well with plastic wrap and freeze. Top with toasted almonds just before serving.

Ahead of time: These can be prepared several weeks ahead if you have space to store them in your freezer.

Tip: Hush! Hush! Your friends will never know how easy it was to produce this superb dessert if you don't tell them.

Cantaloupe with Port

small ripe cantaloupes
port (the best you can afford)

Cut the melons in half. (If you have the time, scallop the edges to make them especially attractive.) Cover and chill briefly. Before serving fill each half with some of the port; pass the port bottle at the table so that each guest can take more if he or she likes.

Tip: This is an exciting first course too.

Frozen Truffle Merriment

[serves 6]

½ pound dark sweet
  chocolate

1 quart chocolate ice cream
12 candied cherries

Chop the chocolate coarsely; it should be in pieces about the size of small peas. Form the ice cream into 6 balls, putting 2 candied cherries in the center of each. Freeze for a short time, then roll in the chopped chocolate and return to freezer until time to serve.

Ahead of time: If you plan to store these in the freezer for more than 24 hours, wrap them in plastic wrap.

Tip: If you pass a bowl of whipped cream with this dessert, you may be surprised to see how many guests will gild this lily.

Fruit Compote, Oranged Easily

[serves about 8]

1 (1-pound, 14-ounce) can peach halves

1 (1-pound, 14-ounce) can apricot halves

1 (1-pound, 14-ounce) can pitted Bing cherries

grated rind and juice of 2 oranges

grated rind and juice of 1 lemon

½ cup brown sugar (pack to measure)

Drain off all the liquid from the canned fruit; save for other purposes. Arrange the fruit in a casserole with peaches on the bottom, next the apricots, then the cherries. Sprinkle with the grated rinds and juice of oranges and lemon. Top with the brown sugar. Bake uncovered at 375° for about 30 minutes. Serve hot or cold.

Ahead of time: This can be prepared the day before. Serve cold or reheat and serve warm.

Tip: Nice to serve either with whipped cream or with a pitcher of heavy cream (unwhipped).

Index